Sonya knew and remembered me from my young childhood at church, although my first memories of her come from my teenage years where she and her husband, Joe, served in the youth at a local church. At the time she had two young boys. She taught piano, served in the church, and cared for her husband, children, and anyone else that needed her. Sonya has a degree in education, but chose to devote her time to her Lord, husband, and children. Oh, how that was such the right choice. Sonya epitomizes the Christian women: she puts God first, her husband second, and children third. Sonya and Joe counseled my husband and I before we were married. I still have the papers she hand-wrote for me to put in my Bible. She knew what I would need because she had lived it first. Oh, how many times I have gone back to those teachings. She showed me ways to structure my time, save on groceries, and ways to pray for my husband and future children (we now have four boys just like her and Joe. Doesn't God know just who we need in our lives to go before us to counsel us!) Not only is Sonya beautiful on the inside, but on the outside as well. Her countenance is radiant, a sure sign of what's within. God tells the "older" women to teach the younger. There is no one more suitable for this than my dear Sonya.

Erin Laxton,

*wife, mother of four boys and educator*

Someone once said, "A woman who embraces her faith and love for Jesus with open arms has the power to inspire others to do the same." I feel this quote directly describes my sister, Sonya. In the 41 years I have known her, I know of her strong desire to help others and I know her love for Christ is unmistakable. Whether it is leading or teaching music, singing, working with youth groups, helping young mothers and families, counseling newlyweds, and more – I know this is truly what the Lord has called my sister to do. Single women, newlyweds, and mothers all alike will benefit from reading my sister's book. It is a heartfelt and inspiring testament of Sonya's unwavering love for Christ and her commitment to living a life full of faith and love. It offers readers a glimpse into her personal journey and the lessons she's learned along the way. With a focus on our relationship with God and personal growth, this book will help any woman seeking to deepen her spiritual connections and strengthen her relationship with God. I feel that it will also help anyone live a more intentional life, guided by faith and allow you to embrace your unique purpose with confidence and grace. I am so proud of my sister and I hope you will take the time to read her devotional. I know it will encourage you, just as it has me.

Wendy Parker,
*wife, mother of three and educator*

Proverbs 31:26 describes Sonya Storey better than any words I could put together myself. "She openeth her mouth with wisdom; and in her tongue is the law of kindness." Sonya is the inspiration and example that all young women need in their lives. I know when I receive advice, or just a word of encouragement, that it is always done through the love of Christ. How she models Jesus in her daily life is enough to change lives forever. I am eternally grateful to have such a role model in my life and my daughters' lives.

Shaee Bolton,
*wife, mother of five daughters, owner of Goodly Heritage Greater Goods*

# PLANT
## —ON—
## PURPOSE
### LIVE A LIFE WITHOUT REGRET

SONYA R. STOREY

# PLANT
# ON
# PURPOSE

*Plant on Purpose*
Copyright© 2023 by Sonya Storey

Library of Congress Cataloging-in-Publication Data

Library of Congress Number: 2023911447 ISBN: 978-1-961732-11-7 (ebook) | ISBN: 978-1-961732-04-9 (paperback) | ISBN: 978-1-961732-05-6 (print)

Published in association with Called Creatives Publishing, www.calledcreativespublishing.com

*Cover design: Called Creatives Publishing*
*Interior design: Sonya Storey*

2023 – First Edition

# Dedication

To my Joe, my sweetheart, greatest supporter, and best friend. Thank you for your constant encouragement and understanding. You are the catalyst for all this, and I am honored to be your wife, walking beside you on this life journey!

To the Storey Boys, you are my most incredible legacy! I am proud to be your mom, and I am so excited to see you continue to grow into great godly men.

To my mom for the love, prayers, and guidance you've given me all my life. Your wisdom and constant positivity have been instrumental!

To my daddy, whose citizenship is in Heaven now, for raising me to believe that anything I dream of is possible!

Finally, to my precious friend Myrian. This book would still be a dream without you.

# Table of Contents

# Foreword

Sonya Storey and I met when our husbands were studying for the ministry, and we have prayed for one another through the changing seasons of our lives. I am delighted to introduce her first book, *Plant on Purpose: Living a Life without Regret,* because it expresses the passion of Sonya's life to plant seeds in her own life, in the lives of her family, and in the lives of many others. Sonya's compassion has overflowed into the lives of infants, toddlers, children, teens, and women.

After moving through her difficulty of infertility to her blessing of mothering four boys, she always called her boys her "gifts from heaven." She intentionally set aside a season in her life to home educate the boys despite many who spoke discouragement into her days. I remember her delight when moving from preschool to kindergarten for the first time. She exclaimed, "Homeschooling is a real treat!" After years of discouraging comments from those who should have encouraged, multiple family health emergencies, and a house fire, when asked once more, "How do you live every day with so many boys?" Sonya replied, "The Lord and Legos are my secret." She intentionally planted seeds with her focus on the future harvest in her sons rather than on the present difficulties.

Sonya deliberately set her goals to make a difference in the lives of people here and the souls of people for eternity:

- teaching parenting classes to families with special needs

babies

- helping her boys speak out to policy makers in education
- giving her time to help those in desperate situations
- scattering encouraging words via notes, texts, and emails
- sharing Christ and His truths with Sunday school classes of all ages

The Apostle Paul quotes a proverb in 2 Corinthians 9:6 when he says, "He which soweth sparingly shall reap also sparingly; and he which soweth bountifully shall reap also bountifully." Sonya has planted seeds in lives at several churches during our friendship. At each new ministry, she asks that I "pray daily for her as she opens her heart and soul to these new people." Then as God answers that prayer, and the seeds begin to sprout in their lives, I hear her exclaim, "I am so happy serving here and being used for the glory of God."

As you begin to read this book, it is my prayer that you will practice watering the seeds that mean the most to you and that your life of intentionality will reap a blessed harvest.

Erica Messer
April 3, 2023

# A Word from the Author

"Son, if you want to go to the moon, we will build you the Rocketship." This phrase has been echoed through the halls of our home since our sons were very young. We even purchased small rocket ship magnets, wooden trinkets, and other accessories to pepper throughout our house to remind them to "Dream Big." Whatever they dreamed, their dad and I would make it happen. They dreamed of learning musical instruments, and it happened. They wanted to raise chickens, meet authors of their favorite books, meet musicians, hike, do professional bike riding, and play college sports; it all happened! Did these dreams come true because they vocalized them? No! Goals were set with intention.

We saved money, and long hours of sweat, hard work, and dedication always followed. Sometimes as women, we forget what life was like before marriage, children, or our younger rambunctious selves. Sometimes setting goals and fulfilling dreams seem more like something that cannot be attained. They may seem misplaced in our piles of laundry, on our never-ending "to-do list," or even daily life expectations. However, no matter our age or stage, we can shoot for the stars, build our rocket ship with the desires God has already placed in our minds, and blast off to become the person we want to be. Since reading this book, I know you are ready to stop living your life with the "best of intentions" and are prepared to strap your boots on and head to the moon. For years I avoided sharing my writings in a published book. My fear and anxieties of being vulnerable for the world to view were almost unbearable. However, after a season filled with pain and disappointments, blessings, and restorations, I know I can no longer keep these words I have penned for years from being shared. I desire to share with young women, wives, and mothers the intentions, systems, and routines that have withstood the test of time in our home. They are bursting forth with great anticipation. They are ready to be shared with future generations of women. The Lord placed this book within me many years ago. By reading, I've come to this conclusion. The older I get, the more I realize that Jesus doesn't want my agreement; He wants my action. The following pages are my actions. May the things I share with you encourage your journey as an intentional woman who will change the world! My heart is igniting with a passion for inspiring and serving you throughout the pages ahead.

Strap your boots on.

Here we go.

3-2-1

Blast off!

# Introduction

Have you ever filled a cheap, recycled plastic grocery bag with too many canned goods, and the bottom fell out? Or, bust a bag holding a gallon of milk? I must be honest; waiting on the "clean up" crew was messy and embarrassing. This happens daily when we, as women, try to do it all. We end up busting our bubble under pressure, maybe even losing our temper or being snappy at those we love the most because we have filled our bags with too heavy items.

As a woman, whether a wife, a mother, or a single gal, you cannot do everything. Living intentionally removes a few of the "too heavy" items in our bags so we can carry only what is necessary. Like Mary and Martha in scripture, we need to become like Mary and choose the "good parts that will not be taken away" (Luke 10:42). Many people walk around with meaningless lives. They seem to be half-awake, even when busy doing what they think is essential. Sometimes they are like Martha, packing too much in their plastic bag.

The way we get meaning out of life is to live intentionally, serving Christ, loving others, being devoted to the community, and creating something that gives us purpose and meaning--- an intentional life! Living with a deliberate mindset is a way of thinking that becomes a learned habit. The intentional mindset is purposeful and committed to the overall goal of having an impact on your life and those lives around you. When you have a more significant direction and purpose, you know exactly where to invest your time and attention.

This book is not a set of instructions but a path I've taken my whole life. Routines are the key to life. Just as a seed won't grow into a beautiful flower overnight, intentional living is a life that blooms and blossoms over time, requiring water, attention, and care. Like a wrestling match, life is a series of pulling back and forth. We know what we need to do, but we often neglect others or take our time here on earth for granted, even though we know we shouldn't ever take anything for granted.

Life is short. Death is certain. Dying is the one thing most of us ignore or try to forget. However, at the end of your days, what will you regret? Many will pass away without ever taking a risk or living out the life God intended for them to live. The thought of this is unbearable to me. Your life will overflow with unspeakable joy, and the generations that come after you will continue speaking of the purposeful life you lived! Begin right now by living today as if this is your last day on earth: Develop a plan, dance to the music, take a walk with a friend, create a list of activities you would like to explore, sit down, and have conversations, say prayers, sing songs, and engage in intentional interactions.

This book will cheer you on as you journey through the days and years ahead. Your life as a woman is a beautiful story. Your life is a book written as a legacy for future generations. People "read" our story from the way we engage with culture. Enlightening them to see what the Christian walk is all about. Today is another chapter, and this book will help you to write that book well.

# Chapter 1

## Spiritual Life - Water the Seeds of Your Faith

*For I will pour water upon him that is thirsty, and floods upon the dry ground: I will pour my spirit upon thy seed, and my blessing upon thine offspring. – Isaiah 44:3*

*Intention is one of the most potent forces in the universe.* If we want to experience the incredible power and direction of the Lord leading us daily, intention doesn't happen by accident. Without this event, no matter how many times you read the Bible, are a good person, or even pray, all this is in vain without a personal relationship with Jesus. To be intentional and grow in your faith, you must have a relationship with Jesus to grow in that faith. The Bible declares that you must surrender control to the Lord, believe in your heart that Jesus died on the cross to pay your penalty for sin, and believe God has raised Him from the dead (Romans 10:9).

Has there ever been a moment in your life where you have prayed, repented of your sin, or placed your faith and trust in Jesus?

Do you believe in him for your salvation from sin? Do you read the Bible, study it, and follow its instructions? If not, nothing listed above will have spiritual benefits for you. You can do everything the Bible commands, but if you do not have a personal relationship with Him, all this is meaningless. You can do that now if you have not received Jesus' gift of salvation. You can pray like this: "Father, I thank you that Jesus died for my sins. I believe He arose from the grave and paid the price for my salvation. I surrender my life to you, believing Jesus died and rose again. I ask that you forgive me of my sin and save me, so heaven is my home when I die."

Amen.

## Seed of Bible Reading

Walking with the Savior is so important. In starting your faith walk, you will experience the Lord's direction in your life in ways you could have never anticipated. If you are wondering how to walk with Jesus as one in a relationship with Him, I want to share how I walk with Him. I start my day by being intentional with time with my Savior by reading my Bible, writing scripture, praying, and listening to worship music. Meeting Him every day is my sacred morning practice. It makes all the difference in how I journey throughout my day.

Earlier in my life, a professor shared a quote by missionary Hudson Taylor: "Do not have your concert first and tune your instruments afterward. Begin the day with prayer and Bible study." While I strive to live each day as if it is my last day on earth, I find that a morning routine or rhythm is the key. Here's my practice: I sit in a particular seat and have my journal, books, highlighters, prayer book, etc., in a basket nearly. If you want to be a woman who follows Jesus and lives an abundant life, as we read in John 10:10, here are some tools to help you. These seeds of faith are actions we cultivate every day. By reading our Bible, we are planting these seeds of faith. When we live intentionally, we live out the truths we read and practice every day. We are demonstrating in front of a world without Christ what we believe. These actions water the seeds of faith. Some days are harder to water than others. When this happens, we must move forward.

With every fiber of my being, I believe our lifeline is woven into our connection to Jesus (Matthew 6:6, Hebrews 4:16). *The secret to abundance is to want what God wants.* Are we perfect? No, but if we have trusted in

> *The secret to abundance is to want what God wants.*

Jesus, we are forgiven. Each day is a new gift. This is why it is called the present. If we fail, which we often do, we must return and start again. Failure is never final with God! Hebrews 13:8 says, "He is the same yesterday, today, and forever." He still is the merciful God that shut the lions' mouths for Daniel in the Old Testament. Philippians 4:6-7 tells us not to be anxious over anything. We fail, and we get back up. Throughout scripture, God uses broken things. Scripture reminds us in Psalm 103:12 that our sins are removed as far as the East is from the West. When we have setbacks, and it's a given, we will. They are just that. A setback is not a campsite. We don't pack a bag and camp out there. A setback is a setback. Move forward. Plead with Him to grant you what He wants to give you! Ask Him for forgiveness and move forward, planning to water your seeds.

## Seed of Writing Scripture and Prayer

I have a journal where I write a new scripture every morning while drinking my coffee. This journal establishes a routine of reading and hiding the word in my heart, and I'm also filling pages with handwritten scriptures to hand down to the next generation. Acts 17:28 says in Him we live and move and have our being. Those who come after me will see how important the word of God is/ was to me. The scripture you write can be displayed on notecards or sticky notes and placed by the kitchen sink or refrigerator door. Watering the seeds is not something time-consuming or elaborate. Watering happens during your daily routines. You can create your scripture writing each month or find several printouts online to enhance your everyday life. Either way, the word of God will come alive as you invest your moments daily with Jesus.

Finally, being intentional in your prayer life will transform you in ways you could not imagine. In seventh grade, my parents taught me how to compose a prayer journal and begin praying for individuals and their needs by name each day. Lest you think a prayer list/journal is a Letter to Santa List to God, it is not. A prayer list is specific prayers for His will for others: seeds or anything we'd like to talk to God about as we go through life.

Throughout the years, I have encouraged our sons and others in our ministries to "pray so big and so often that when Jesus meets you at Heaven's gate, He says with a smile, "Kid, you kept me very busy." Write down the request people ask of you. Suppose you can't write them down, email them, or text them yourself. You can even put them in a note on your phone. I email myself around 20 emails daily of important things I need to pray about and people to pray with and for. You also do not have to wait and pray later. If you are with the person when they share their request, take a moment and pray out loud with them before your conversation is over. Scripture tells us we have not because we ask not (James 4:2). James teaches us that if we have the right motives within us, He will answer. Does this mean that God will give you whatever you ask for? Not necessarily. Sometimes His answer is "Yes, no, or not right now." Micah 7:7 encourages us to "Wait on Him." When we have the right desires and walk by faith, He will never fail us.

I keep a quote from evangelist George Mueller throughout our house. He was a Christian evangelist in the 1800s and director of the Ashley Down orphanage in Bristol, England. He said, "Be assured, if you walk with Him and look to Him, and expect help from Him, He will never fail you." Throughout his life, George cared for over 10,000 orphans, providing them with educational opportunities. He established 117 schools that offered Christian education to more than 120,000 students. His autobiography records that they had no provisions once the children ate breakfast. Still, Mr. Mueller said the blessing over the meal and thanked the Lord for how He would provide for them today. Almost immediately, a knock was at the door. It was the baker. He said he could not sleep because he was sure the Lord wanted him to bake bread for the children. Mueller told the children that they not only had bread for breakfast but fresh bread. He offered the milk to the children, completing their meal! Almost immediately, another knock came. This time it was the milkman; the cart had broken down outside the orphanage.

When we neglect to pray and worry about our needs or circumstances instead, this is thinking that God won't get it right. He is with and for us and directs our paths intentionally through our daily decisions. Often we use prayers like a 9-1-1 call or a spare tire. Praying is a daily privilege, and we should talk to our Father. Imagine if your child never spoke to you until they wanted something. This is how the Lord feels when we neglect time with Him daily.

In 2000, I read a little book called *The Prayer of Jabez* by Bruce Wilkinson. Jabez has been an inspiration to my prayer life. The intent of my prayers has never been the same since taking the challenge to pray like Jabez: Lord blesses me indeed, enlarge my territory, and keep your hand on me and keep me from evil. Some prayers are "yes," some are "no," and some are "not right now."

11

Becoming intentional with your prayer life will reap a harvest of unanswered and answered prayers. *Become a woman who trusts God's plan, even when you don't understand.*

*Become a woman who trusts God's plan, even when you don't understand.*

## Seed of Spiritual Encouragement
### *Worship Music*

Next, grow your faith by listening to worship music every day. Consider making a playlist on a device of songs that will encourage you as you go about your day. You can listen to this music as you start your day by putting your make-up on, packing lunches, or commuting to work. If you are working from home or if staying at home with your little ones is your work, plan a few times throughout the day to listen to music. One of my favorites, often on repeat, is "Words I Would Say" by Sidewalk Prophets. Music is a beautiful expression of our spiritual growth. Music prepares your heart to focus on the things of God. The enemy flees when we include worshipful music in our daily routines. When you schedule your spirit for the day's battle with worshipful music, the enemy flees.

## Seed of Spiritual Growth
### *Church Attendance*

Finally, grow your faith by regularly attending church. Take your children to church, even when it's hard to juggle and seems like it is wasting your time. Trust me. It is not a waste of time. More is caught than taught. I have met many mothers at church services who encouraged my family and me to walk with Him. Being a mom and walking the path of motherhood sometimes is just simply showing up at church. At times in my life, I had no idea what I was doing as a mother, but being present where other believers were and worshiping the Lord through a local church helped me. When you have a sweet spirit and a happy attitude, your little ones will soon enjoy attending Sunday school, AWANA, youth group, etc. These services will be woven into their memories, and as they grow up, the church will become as precious to them as it is to us.

We need the church as we strive to make good choices, build community and relationships with others, and share our faith by inviting others to attend with us. James 4:17 says that when we know to do good or right and don't do it, it is a sin. This is a gentle reminder that we all need a local church. Jesus died for the church (Ephesians 5:25). Building relationships is a part of the Christian life. Cultivate godly relationships. Share your faith by telling others what Jesus means to you. Romans 10:14-15 reminds us that beautiful are the feet of those who bring the good news. Imagine if someone had not told you about Jesus. He is our hope for Heaven.

Be strong and keep the faith. God has His hand on your life. Never forget this. Faith makes things possible, not easy. Make time to read your Bible, pray, write and live scripture, and listen to uplifting music. When your heart and mind are quiet, you can hear His voice. Open up to His presence to fill you with fuel- the Holy Spirit for this crazy life. Ephesians 3:16-19 says he will strengthen you with power through his Spirit in your inner being. May you feel His strength and presence.

## Seed of Daily Commitment

Our desire as Christian women should be to live a whole life trusting in the promises of God. Planning daily time with Jesus, praying, listening to worship songs, and hiding the Word in our hearts by writing out scripture, will allow the Holy Spirit to grow you into the woman He destined you to become. We may teach what we know, but we will produce how we live. Live and grow spiritually by watering the seeds that matter most to us daily. Psalm 90:12 says, "So teach us to number our days that we may apply our hearts to wisdom." Prayerfully planning our days lets us stay focused on what is essential. Proverbs 4:23 reminds us to keep our heart with all diligence, for out of it are issues or sources of life. First and foremost, being intentional about our relationship with Jesus takes preeminence over everything we could ever plan or do.

2 Timothy 1:9 reminds us that the Lord knows those who are his. He loves us. God desires to make each of His children in the image of Jesus. When we are intentional in meeting Him every day, before we start the rhythms of the day, we are making Him a priority. Your Christian life is not a matter of "having the time" or something that hinders your walk with God. It is a matter of what you prioritize the most. When we prioritize time with Him, we will reap the benefits (peaceful life, stronger faith, joy, contentment, wisdom, vision for the future, ways to handle this crazy world, etc.). Reading His word daily and prioritizing time with Him will drastically change how you view every day of your life. However, reading or studying the Bible, attending church, etc., won't cause a Christian to grow spiritually. Just as if sitting in a garage won't make you a car. Living out the word of God by the words we speak to others, by our daily actions, moment by moment, and situation by situation causes spiritual growth.

**List three ways you can water these seeds each day:**

*We plant, we water, we wait, and then we harvest! Water the seeds that mean the most to you!*

# Chapter 2

Behavior – Water the Seeds of a Godly Life

*Pursue righteousness, godliness, faith, love, patience, gentleness.*
*– I Timothy 6:11 ESV*

Every day we should strive to passionately pursue a good and godly life: an authentic life that is faithful to Jesus and transparent to those around us. In this chapter, we will see where to start if you want to live a Godly life. We represent the kingdom of God with our choices, behavior, etiquette, and words. We are the only Bible many women will ever "read or see." How we live as single women, wives, or mothers leaves an imprint on the hearts of those we encounter. So, we want to plant the Godly seeds of encouragement, kindness, and habits as we go about our days.

## Seeds of Encouragement

I Thessalonians 5:11 tells us to "Encourage one another and build each other up." Romans 15:2 tells us to please our neighbors to build them up for their good. Think about how you make others feel when they talk with you. Consider the lady at the grocery store pick-up or the gentleman at the restaurant; how you interact with and speak to those you meet in ordinary, everyday spaces matters. You have the opportunity to shine brightly and share the hope that is within you.

I try each day to encourage one person. That's it—just one. But once I encourage one person, I encourage many more throughout my day. Your words of encouragement have power. Consider this Maya Angelou quote: "People will forget what you said. People will forget what you did. But people will never forget how you made them feel."

When we choose encouraging words, it lifts others. Words are powerful. And those words are influenced by how you think. Let's think about what we are thinking about. When we feel good encouraging thoughts, the words that come from our heads and hearts are more likely to bless others.

All of this begins in our minds, where we cultivate a godly life. Every day we need to weed the garden of our minds. Ask the Lord to take every thought captive (2 Corinthians 10:5), guarding our lips to only speak wholesome words. Proverbs 4:23 says to guard your heart, for out of it are the issues of life. Let's refuse today to let trash enter our minds or leave our mouths.

This is only one of the many good choices we can make. Choices are essential; our choices and reactions to individuals and situations soon become our behavior. Practiced behaviors then become a habit. Habits have the potential to become a blessing and change your life! Good habits are part of a godly life. These habits do not have to come from a complete overhaul of our personalities or lives; minor daily adjustments can transform you. If we want to change our lives and live a life of purpose, we must break old habits and begin living each day to its full potential.

As you read this chapter, it would be best not to feel discouraged or defeated. We all mess up. Isaiah 54:10 reminds us that God's kindness won't depart us. When you fail to speak words of encouragement or develop a new habit, you will not allow failure to become your story. Defeat is never final with God. You must view each day as a present from the Lord. Unwrap it and begin living life without regrets!

Take a moment to look up and listen to Brandon Heath's song "Give Me Your Eyes." This song is powerful. I cannot look at the individuals I encounter daily without thinking of the artist's words.

## Seed of Behavior

One event that I do habitually is weekly planning. When our sons were young children, they took naps every Sunday afternoon. As they got older, we made a routine of F.O.B. (i.e., Flat On Bed). Each boy could take a book, draw, etc., and stay in their room to encourage rest. Rest is vital not only for women but families. Sunday afternoon sabbath, as I liked to call it, is still essential to my routine now as an almost empty nester. So, after the Sunday church service and lunch were cleaned up, we rested. In my resting, I sit down and plan out the following week- seven full days. I schedule menus, appointments, church, church activities, music lessons, sports, etc.

I always include one or two days where self-care is planned. My schedule is intentional and set. However, it is always flexible. I add a few items from my 3-6 and 12-month goal planning list and strive to be productive daily. These goals can be as simple as eliminating clutter in my house by donating five unused items daily and placing them in the donation box. I also eliminate unnecessary or non-worn clothing items, books not read, or anything that can reduce visible clutter in my house. I have one rule about clutter:

"Everything has a home." I don't postpone anything that can be done in 5 minutes or less. If I get something out, I put it up. It also means I tidy up in the evenings before bed. Performing this helps my emotional well-being and is a part of my daily self-help moving checklist. My motivation is this: Today could be my last day on earth; make it count! Think about it. What would you be doing if you knew today was your last day? Scripture asks us in James 4:14, "What is life?" He then reminds us that it is a vapor that appears for a short time and then vanishes away. Make today count!

Daily, take care of yourself spiritually with Bible reading and studying, journaling, and prayer time. Try to spend time without your phone; it may seem impossible, but trust me, this investment is worth it! I try not to touch my phone in the morning until I have spent time with the Lord. I am super mindful of setting time limitations on all social media outlets. I also prioritize caring for something other than the husband, children, and home. I enjoy watching for our dogs, plants, and small garden. Helping something else grow and thrive is rewarding and allows me to manage my stress.

Let me explain. Ephesians 4:32 tells us to be kind to one another. Often we want to change the world by building buildings or providing a massive financial donation to a cause. Nothing is wrong with either of these ideas, but *a single act of kindness can change everything.* People are often one decision from a different life. Likewise, people are one person from a different life.

*a single act of kindness can change everything.*

Kindness matters! Most people desire human contact—a natural person to speak life into them. One kind word is all they need to have the strength to keep moving forward in their day.

Your random acts of kindness do make a difference. We may not see this side of Heaven, but it does. Here are a few suggestions on how we can sew the seed of kindness into our everyday routines:

- Give a homeless person a meal.
- Smile at someone.
- Ask the cashier about their favorite candy bar or gum. Add that to your purchase and give it to them as you exit.
- Tip the coffee employees at the coffee shops and drive-thru.
- Leave those who pick up your trash weekly with water or a snack.
- Take a box of donuts to the police department.
- Place food in your local Blessing Box.

Be friendly. Be kind. But most importantly, be honest. Demonstrate the love of Jesus through your actions. Religion repels love lures. When an individual leaves our presence, they should see evidence of Jesus' love through our seeds of words and actions, knowing that we are different.

Our youngest son is preparing to go away to college. We have met many coaches and toured multiple athletic programs. On one particular visit, we met Coach Scotty Walden, who said, "How you do something is how you do everything. We must do our work as we are working for the Lord. No matter how we feel." *As women, we must learn to live beyond the way we feel.* Somedays, I do not feel like a Christian. I may hit my toe on the dresser at 5 a.m. or step on a Lego in the middle of the night. How much do we let our feelings control all

> *As women, we must learn to live beyond the way we feel.*

our emotions, good or bad? Or, what do we say or do? Remember Ephesians 4:26 and practice being angry but not sinning.

Think about this for a moment. In truth, we act the way we feel, not feel the way we act. Our actions reveal what is going on inside our minds. The utmost part of our being is demonstrated through our efforts. Deuteronomy 33:25 tells us that as our days, so shall our strength be. There is strength for every season of life. This means that no matter what we go through, we will have the power to deal with it. We must look to Him for all we need and watch what He will do.

## Seed of Practice

Finally, remember these words I share with my piano students: Practice makes permanent, not perfect! Get better every day at becoming the best version of yourself! More often than we say, we will do something challenging or unique but never do. Instead of practicing all these seeds listed in this chapter to better our lives, we procrastinate and expect life will get easier after that one thing. After this season, after the holidays, the wedding, the funeral, the birthday party, etc., life will get easier. After we hit the goal after we make more money after we move into a new house or new neighborhood, life will get easier. After finals, I'll go to Bible study, and after graduation, things will get easier for me to attend church or volunteer in my community. After the kids are out of the house, after we retire, and after our parents are in our home, life will be easier.

Here's a wonderful tip for you to remember: Things will never get easier! So, what is a woman to do? We must learn to handle it harder. Practicing this allows our brain to have a mental shift. It will never happen if we walk around waiting for things to get easier. Life is hard! Mothering is hard. Being a woman is hard. When is it going to get easy? It's not! The second God sees us practicing and handling hard better, He will often make it harder. Why? He is preparing us for the next big steps in life. We are deceiving ourselves if we think life will suddenly get easier because we have attained or birthed a child, obtained a degree, or written a book. *Make yourself a woman who handles hard well.* Not a woman who looks for the easy. Have a meaningful pursuit in life.

*Make yourself a woman who handles hard well.*

**What words or actions can you do today to make a difference in someone's life?**

*We plant, we water, we wait, and then we harvest! Water the seeds that mean the most to you!*

# Chapter 3

## Self-Care – Water the Seeds of Personal Well-Being

*Blessed is the man (or woman) whose trust is in the LORD, whose trust is the LORD; he is like a tree planted by water, that sends out its roots by the stream, and does not fear when heat comes, for its leaves remain green, and is not anxious in the year of drought, for it does not cease to bear fruit. – Jeremiah 17:7-8 KJV*

Self-care is the simple practice of caring for yourself. It means protecting and safeguarding your well-being. In my life, these areas are spiritual, physical, mental, and emotional. I have recommendations here, but remember, you can only decide what self-care means! Establish what this is and guard it.

The Bible clearly states that we must take time and care for ourselves to draw near Him. In Psalm 46:5, God says he is within us and will help us. Ephesians 2:10 says, "You are God's handiwork, created in Christ Jesus to do good work which God prepared in advance for us to do." Similarly, Isaiah 64:8 reminds us that we are the clay, and He is the potter. We are all the work of His hands.

The Bible does not directly say "self-care is needed," but "take care of yourself" is written many times.

A few examples of how Jesus took time to rest and care for His soul are listed in a few of my favorite scriptures:

- Mark 12:31 - "Love your neighbor as you love yourself."
- I Timothy 5:8 - "Jesus even took time out of his busy day to rest."
- Luke 5:16 - "Jesus withdrew himself into the wilderness and prayed."

Remember, you are not wasting time when you are resting because you are exhausted. You are doing exactly what you need to do. You are recovering. Isaiah 30:15 reminds us that in returning and rest, you shall be saved; in quietness, trust shall be your strength. We must take time out for rest and care for the body He has given us.

Self-care is more than going to great lengths to maintain physical appearance. While you can include these things in your routine, this is not the goal. Each day we have hours to work, be a caregiver, and other hours to do the things required of us. We must not forget about ourselves as we journey through life.

Scripture tells us in Psalm 37: 23-24 that the Lord orders the steps of a good man (or woman). Even though He orders our efforts, we must make choices every day. If we take good care of ourselves, we will alleviate unnecessary stress or hardships that typically follow when living in chaos. Think about this: Each day, we are becoming the books we read, the movies we watch, the music we listen to, the people we spend time with, and the conversations we engage in. We choose wisely what we feed our mind and the time we use to care for ourselves. When you prioritize taking care of yourself, you can bless others with your kindness and positive attitude because in taking care of yourself, you can appropriately take care of others without unnecessary stress or hardship.

Psalms 16:11 reminds us that He will show us the path of life and that in His presence is fullness of joy. This path cannot be revealed if we are too busy to slow down or pause to be in His presence before we face the day's challenges. This verse is a beautiful example of time management and timing to be in His presence. When we fill our souls with the care of our body, soul, and spirit, this enhances our self-confidence, increases productivity and happiness, helps us live well, and improves physical, mental, and spiritual health.

## Seeds of Saying "No"

Peace will follow when we are intentional about our daily steps and desire to walk in His presence. Aligning your needs with God's will, not the desire of others, will create a blank space in your calendar, giving you time to grow and cultivate your dreams and desires. You will then begin to see sprouts of new possibilities with a fruitful bounty in the months and years ahead. Beware that living where boundaries are present may cause others to get irritated or frustrated. Sometimes we may have to say "no" to extra activities that are not on our agenda for the season of life we are in. I am not telling you not to take cookies to the PTA meeting or snacks to the church nursery. But I remind you that "no" is not a four-letter word. It's ok to say no. I had to learn this the hard way. In my life, I want to focus and give attention to every present task, but in recognizing the needs of others, I must keep my eyes on Jesus and fervently seek His direction to what I say "yes" to all the extra things in my daily life.

## Seeds of Planning

Every Sunday afternoon, I sit down and plan out the following week. I schedule menus, appointments, church, church activities, music lessons, sports, etc. My schedule is intentional and set. However, it is always flexible. I add a few items from my 3-6-month and 12-month goal planning list and strive to be productive daily. My motivation is this: Today could be my last day on earth. Make it count! *As long as I'm still here, there is more ahead of me to do.* Think about one

> *As long as I'm still here, there is more ahead of me to do.*

new thing you would like to learn. Maybe, it is learning to play the piano online or from an instructor. Make plans and do it! Perhaps it's learning a second language. We have more access now to enrichment classes online, so there are not any excuses to give for not enriching your life. May you need to set goals, read a self-help book, go to counseling for past hurts, or even attend a ladies' Bible study group to enhance your knowledge of scripture. Whatever it is, start today. A dream written down with a date becomes a goal. A goal broken down into steps becomes a plan. A plan backed by actions will soon become a reality.

## Seed of Small Indulgences

Treat yourself like someone you love. When I make time for facials, paint my nails, fix myself up by wearing my favorite lip gloss, or improve my self-talk by playing a song that inspires me to push forward, I am doing what is best for me, even if it is less than an hour a week. When you do this, you will find all kinds of spaces in your day to pour into the people you love the most.

Here are a few self-care suggestions that have worked for me.

- **Prioritize and set realistic goals that work best for you and your family.** Be mindful that as children grow

and seasons in life change, so do your self-care needs.
I spent time with Jesus during their naps when our
sons were very young. As they grew older and outgrew
naps, I began getting up earlier.

- **Spend time without your phone.** This may seem
impossible, but this investment is worth gold! I strive
not to touch my phone in the morning until I have
spent time with the Lord. I am super mindful (thanks
to my youngest son) of setting time limitations on
all social media outlets. Another avenue I prioritize
and enjoy is taking care of something other than your
immediate family (i.e., husband, children, and home).
These things are a given. Find one or two things that
are something you enjoy. I enjoy reading, taking care
of our dogs, scrapbooking, playing the piano, and
discussing the maintenance of household plants and
my small garden. Helping something else grow and
thrive is rewarding and allows me to manage my stress.
So, I am super intentional in planning and making
daily time for these things. Realistically, I cannot do
all these things every day, but I can plan to pepper
these self-care exercises throughout my week on my
weekly planning sheets. I've always said, "Ink is better
than my memory."

- **Put reminders on your phone or another method
that best suits your personality.** Keep this time a
priority, just like an appointment. When you practice
this mindset, it doesn't make you perfect. It just
makes it permanent. Practice makes it permanent,
not perfect. If something happens and you don't have
time, get back up the next day and move forward. Too
many times, I beat myself up about failures. Become a

woman who takes care of herself as well as pours into the lives of others.

## Seeds of Rest

There are over a dozen scripture references that tell us to rest. Here are a few of my favorites:

- Exodus 20:8
- Exodus 33:14
- Psalm 4:8
- Psalms 23:2-3
- Psalm 127:1-2
- Proverbs 3:21-24
- Jeremiah 6:16
- Matthew 11:28-30
- Hebrews 4:9-1

Jesus himself even took time to rest. John 6:3 tells us that he went up to the mountain and sat down with his disciples. I believe he sat down and relaxed. In Mark 4:35-40 we see where Jesus was asleep in the boat when a storm came. The disciples woke up and asked Him if He didn't care or not if they drowned. Jesus quietly rose and rebuked the winds and waves, saying, "Peace Be Still." At that moment, everything went calm. We all have things in life that we must do. Rest is one of them. Our most remarkable example rested, so we must too. Jesus knows that it is needful for us to stop and rest. We must prioritize this practice for our souls and future generations. We work hard 5-6 days per week. We must have a day when our family is experiencing an understanding of the importance of resting. Even in the Creation events, God gave us His example of resting on the seventh day. Was He tired and needed a nap? No! He gave us a pattern of how to live full, productive lives, taking care of ourselves physically and self-care.

A few suggestions that help me in the rest area are winding down close to bedtime. Have an excellent bedroom and keep lights as low as possible so your body will wind down to receive the needed rest. Don't start any project that requires you to be alert or think.

Finally, I get ready for bed well before it's bedtime. I prepare my sink in the kitchen; it's clean and ready to be used the following day; the nighttime facial regiment is complete, prayers are said, all clothes are laid out for the next day, etc.

## Seeds of Staying Active

In addition to self-care in our spiritual lives, we must maintain self-care in our physical lives. In my physical self-care routine, sleep is essential. I often share with young mothers that sleep is more important than food. Setting expectations and following through is so important. When educating and raising our boys at home, we would guard an hour each day (when appropriate) for rest, especially on Sunday afternoons. They did not have to sleep per se but did have to be "F.O.B." or, as we would say, "flat on the bed." They could read, journal, color, listen to music or audiobooks, etc.

I would rest with them when they were smaller and naps were in our routine. This practice was hard for me. I would sometimes think of all the things I could get accomplished. However, I had to care for myself so that I could survive the rest of the hours of our day. An older lady once told me, "Babies don't keep!" This phrase has stuck with me all these years. As our sons grow into men, I finally understand her wise words. *We are busy and blessed*

*but must take time to rest!.*     *We are busy and blessed but*
                                   *must take time to rest!*

I take care of my physical self-care needs by:

- **Taking vitamins.** Vitamins are critical to overall health. If you don't take any vitamins, start with a single supplement that will immediately boost your energy level and immune system.

- **Exercising 20 minutes 3 days a week.** Exercise is my least favorite thing to do! However, I find time to read on my exercise bike and pray on the elliptical. When time allows, I enjoy a brisk walk around the track at our local park. Walking triggers the body's relaxation responses and helps reduce stress. You may find other types of exercise activities to be helpful. Find an exercise routine that is right for you.

- **Drinking water.** Water is essential to keeping you hydrated and is nourishing to our bodies. Drinking eight glasses of water daily can be overwhelming or intimidating. Try not to wait until the end of the day and force yourself to drink all the water you missed or try to catch up. Instead, divide and conquer the hydration giant that keeps many feeling blah and unhealthy. I place eight rubber bands around my water bottle to help me prioritize my daily water intake. Each time I empty and refill it, I remove a rubber band. All my bands are removed by late afternoon, and water intake is achieved. Another way to be mindful of drinking water is to always drink water when you dine out. Both your body and budget will appreciate this. I also make popsicles using sugar-free Kool-Aid packets or lemons and limes. Staying hydrated has so many health benefits.

- **Attending appointments.** Visit the doctor for your yearly wellness physical check-ups, mammograms, pap smears, cholesterol bloodwork, dental needs, vision exams, and any other exams you have a family history of should be checked yearly. Use a day planner or the calendar on your phone to balance these things and others as a record in a system you can use and quickly refer to.

- **Staying well-groomed.** Keep your hair trimmed and your clothing unwrinkled (use Downey Wrinkle Release) to help eliminate the daily chaos. We've all had times when someone knocks on our door, or we must urgently leave our home for someone or something, and we look like a mess. Without sounding judgemental or legalistic, our outer appearance reveals so much about our inner testimony. I am not saying we should never have times when we don't get dressed or fixed up. The opposite is true. I strive to have one day a week where I "fast" from make-up, don't get dressed until lunchtime, etc., for my Sabbath Rest. On the other days, I am up and at it, ready to be available to anyone who needs me. Looking halfway decent is not only a gift to yourself but also to those around you. One day a week, I pick out seven outfits with accessories and have them ready to grab and go.

- **Planning ahead.** Almost everything in my daily routine is pre-planned (clothing, menus, etc.) Planning eliminates stress. A stress-free life is worth gold in today's fast pace world.

## Seed of Play

Because our children were home-educated for many years, the library was our home away from home. The library was one trip we made each week. Libraries have kids' activities, allowing me to have at least half an hour or longer of free time. I used this time to read or research things I wanted to learn more about. Similarly, I bring a book everywhere I go. I also taxied the boys around for music lessons. Stay in the car during your child's music, dance, or sports practice. Get lost in a book for a few moments, feeding your brain. I also read while riding my exercise bike. It may seem crazy, but any 30 minutes I have, I use them to enhance my mental capabilities. If you don't have 30 minutes, start with 10 minutes daily.

Playing a game is another way to stay connected. Finding a match on your phone that won't take you away for hours is another way to build your brain. To be transparent, I have never played a game on my phone, but my husband highly recommends this and has science to back up his claims that it does help reduce stress. You can care for yourself by memorizing scripture, working puzzles, playing games, learning a second language, or catching up on world events.

## Seed of Creativity

Hobbies are a great way to relax and spend time for yourself. However, hobbies don't "just happen." They have to be included in your daily routines. When we were growing our family, two women from my church introduced me to scrapbooking. They gently encouraged and modeled the importance of a space where I could create and relax. Hobbies taught me that hobbies are not a waste of time. If you do not have a hobby, it's never too late to learn. Many churches or hobby shops have classes offered to help ignite the spark that is within you. Courses often include art, jewelry making, floral arranging, piano lessons, pottery, or knitting. Having a hobby is purposeful in your mental self-care. God likes seeing us having fun and living a happy life.

## Seeds of Emotional Well-Being

Next is taking care of my emotional well-being. Emotions cannot always be trusted. We must seek the Lord and ask for His guidance and direction. As a woman, allowing our feelings to control our actions is NOT easy. A good practice is to pause after an event has rattled me. I pray, ask for wisdom, and keep my mouth closed. Deuteronomy 29:29 says, "The secret things belong to the Lord our God, but the things revealed belong to us, and our children forever, that we may do all the words of this law."

I know this verse is technically speaking about the exact time of the second coming of Christ, but I believe it also applies to our daily lives. Sometimes we must wait and rely on the Lord to help us control our emotions. I think of the old hymn, "Tis So Sweet." The words say, "Tis so sweet to trust in Jesus, to take Him at His word. to rest upon His promise, to know thus said the Lord. Jesus, Jesus, how I trust Him, how I've proved Him o'er and o'er. Jesus, Jesus, precious Jesus! Oh, for grace to trust Him more". We need more faith as we navigate our emotions.

## Seed of Peace

We often become overwhelmed with life trying to control or restrict our emotions. We desire to control life events and get bent out of shape if our plans are disrupted, or life events shatter our idea of how things should be. I want to encourage you not to fear the future or events unfolding throughout the day. Do not fear the future. Deuteronomy 31:6 reminds us to "Be strong and of a good courage, fear not, nor be afraid of them: for the Lord thy God, he it is that doth go with thee: he will not fail thee, nor forsake thee." *He is perpetual with you, taking care of you. His presence is a forever promise. He is already there.* Having peace and realizing that the

> *He is perpetual with you, taking care of you. His presence is a forever promise. He is already there.*

Holy Spirit doesn't consult with our human schedules, needs, emotions, etc., will help us be open to His directing in our lives. Several verses assure us of His presence and peace:

- Matthew 6:34 ESV - "Therefore do not be anxious about tomorrow, for tomorrow will be anxious for itself. Sufficient for the day is its trouble."
- James 4:13-15 ESV - "Come now, you who say, "Today or tomorrow we will go into such and such a town and spend a year there and trade and make a profit, yet you do not know what tomorrow will bring. What is your life like? For you are a mist that appears briefly and then vanishes. Instead, you ought say, "If the Lord wills, we will live and do this or that."
- John 10:10 - The thief comes only to steal and kill and destroy. I came that they may have life and have it abundantly". Jesus desires for you to live life to its fullest."

**What are two things you would do if you knew this was your last day on earth?**

*We plant, we water, we wait, and then we harvest! Water the seeds that mean the most to you!*

# Chapter 4

Your Marriage – Water the Relationship with Your
Husband

*Many waters cannot quench love, neither can the floods drown it. –*
*Song of Solomon 8:7*

## The Single Woman

If you are a single gal, the things in this chapter may not apply to
your life now. However, always be open to learning and listening
to something that could help you in the future. Pray daily for the
Lord to prepare you for the day you might meet an extraordinary
man who may become your husband. Be specific in your prayers.
Focus on Jesus and follow His ways; someday, if it is the Lord's
will, you two will meet.

The man you choose to be your partner could affect everything.
Think about it. Whom you give your heart to will affect your
mental health, peace of mind, successes, dreams, and tragedies,
how your children will be raised, and so much more. Place your
heart in the hands of God, and He will place it in the hands of a

man who deserves you! You want to marry a man who loves Jesus more than you do, who is kind when no one is watching.

## The Married Woman

I have heard that a "happy wife = happy life." I'm not too fond of this statement, as it seems manipulative. Instead, I like *"happy spouse= happy house."* Both husband and wife should be happy within the home. Yes, wives, we are to submit, which means he has the final decision after you both have discussed a matter (Ephesians 5:22-23 and Colossians 3:18-19). Still, I genuinely believe in relational equity (Luke 6:31, Colossians 3:12, I Corinthians 13:4, Ephesians 4:32, and Matthew 7:12). There have only been a few times in all our years together that I disagreed with my husband, but in prayer and confidence, supported the decision he made for our family. Once it all worked out, and for that, I am thankful. However, a few of those times were correct, but I would never tell my man, "I told you so." I allow the Holy Spirit to work in his heart, which keeps harmony in our home.

> *"happy spouse= happy house."*

Talking to Jesus instead of family members, neighbors, or even your friends will only cause harm. When a matter is over and done, we forget. However, others rarely fail and will often harbor ill feelings toward your husband. Speak carefully, and please, please don't complain about anything you can change. Wives, we are to be the encouragers to him, his cheerleader. Be kind to him, even when you don't feel like it. Love is not a feeling. It is a choice! Never forget that you are your husband's partner. You should have a voice and be able to talk with and discuss anything together, even if you don't get your way. We as a woman are created to stand beside, not beneath nor above, not behind, but beside (Genesis 2:22). Creating harmony in the home takes hard work and tenacity. But it's worth the effort!

I grew up in a family of strong faith. Our faith was not just a Sunday event. It was a 24/7, nonstop, continuous, Jesus-seeking and serving every day of our lives. My parents were students of the Word. I still remember the Bible teachings from Adrian Rodgers, Charles Stanley, and Dennis Rainey with Family Life. Our home was transparent. Even though my "all-in moment" came later in my teen years, at this age, I had a strong desire to live for the Lord and to serve Him with all my heart.

In fifth grade, I remember sitting on the steps outside my classroom after school. As I sat quietly on the top step of the stairs, I heard a still, small voice whisper that I would one day marry a pastor and become a pastor's wife. I didn't share this with anyone. I only wrote it in my diary that night before going to bed. You may think this is goofy and that the Lord would not take time to speak to a 10-year-old girl sitting on a public school stairway, but He did. As I grew older and began to date a few guys from my youth group, I would watch and pray. Several guys that I was interested in were not Christians, so I waited. Some time passed, then I met him. At the time, God had not called him to minister behind a pulpit but in medical school. We did not date right away, but eventually, God made way for our relationship to form.

I will never forget re-meeting my husband, Joe, in college. I say re-meeting because we were in 4th grade together. He was the "playground bully" because he liked having a monopoly over the playground monkey bars. No girls were allowed to play on the monkey bars when Joe and his friends were around without his secret passcode. Since Joe's family moved to Tennessee from out of state during our fourth-grade year, I lost track of him.

During my first year of college, I had the opportunity to meet Joe again through a mutual friend. We reminisced about the year he was at my school over pizza (which he denied the whole monkey bars needing a password). As I made my way to campus, I said, "I will marry this guy someday." No joke! I felt it in my spirit. It took over six months, but we finally went on a double date. The rest is history.

Reflecting on my life, I realize that Joe and I – or any couple with a healthy, happy marriage – did not get there by chance. Those married 5, 10, 20, or even 50 years have sacrificed, forgave, apologized, and persevered. Joe and I learned that to have a strong relationship, we must continue to communicate daily, date one another often, dream together, forgive one another, and refuse to give up one another. Most importantly, we must find fulfillment in Jesus, not one another. This is the essential wisdom I can offer you. I love my husband with every fiber of my being. We are all fallible as humans. However, I love Jesus more. Loving Him gives me the strength and determination to continue staying married. Love fiercely, forgive often, and remain faithful to the promise you made on your wedding day.

## Seeds of Preparation

When we married, Joe was in Bible College after studying pre-med at a state school. When God called him to the ministry, he was all in. He left scholarships, credits, and a secure future his parents paved for him. Since I had no idea what it was like to be married, I wrote over 50 letters to women who had been married for many years. I wrote to the president of the college's wife, pastors' wives, businesswomen, and professors, asking for one or two nuggets of advice. To my surprise, many of the letters contained the same information. It was as if they all got together, discussed their answers, and wrote me back simultaneously. It was amazing to read their wisdom. Each reminded me to be an encourager and to respect him as a man. They reminded me that I was not his mother, so I needed to be mindful of this as our years together grew. I am so grateful I listened to the voice of the Lord and mailed those letters. I had to put my "brave on" and be vulnerable when dropping them in the mail.

Five couples got married around the same time as Joe and I. Each of these couples was in church; three were in Bible college or seminary. Each couple divorced five years or less after their wedding date. We are the only couple still married today. Yet, I do not want this to discourage you. Instead, I want this to encourage you to be deliberate in every area of your marriage, one step at a time, one day at a time, or even five minutes at a time. I hope to encourage you in your journey and equip you with practical ways to strengthen your relationship with your husband. No matter where you are in your stage of marriage, my desire is for you to experience a fun-loving, fulfilling, lifelong Christ-centered marriage.

## Seeds of Passion

Marriage is much like a fire. Whether you've been married several years or are newly married and the fire is not burning too bright, keeping the spark alive is essential. If you've ever started a fire, you know it takes patience and must be sustained once it gets going. Maintaining the original flame is so much easier than creating the fire again. We as women must work hard and be intentional not to forget about our husbands amid crazy, busy days. Many may read, ask, or yell at me, "He needs to be intentional!" I agree. When we, as women, keep our marriage priority and do not get lost in our day-to-day routines or forget about our husbands, our love for one another will continue to grow more profound. He will remain awestruck and delighted to be in your presence. I highly recommend watching the movie "Like Arrows." This movie will add clarity and encouragement to your life!

I'd recommend reading books on the different personalities of men and women, personalities/different types of men, marriage books etc., that encourage you to learn more about each other. These book helped me discover the kind of man I married and made our marriage glorious around year 10. When I began to understand how different we are, our home became a sweeter place—educating myself about how I approached and spoke to him after a long day was a game changer. Realizing oneness is not sameness, and it's okay if we are opposites on almost everything. In reality, opposites do attract.

Making sure my brain is in gear before putting my mouth into motion helped too. Seriously though, the key to being intentional with your husband is never to forget why you grew in love in the first place. After 28 years of marriage, as Ruth Bell Graham did, I can say, "I have never thought about divorce, but murder…."

When I type these words, I can't help but recollect falling and growing in love with him. There have been tough days throughout the past 30+ years of courtship and marriage. But there have also been so many treasured days that my husband loves and adores me. Maybe you have never experienced this in your marriage: Don't give up! If there is no Biblical reason to quit, stay the course and allow the Holy Spirit to work miracles in your life and the lives of your family. Never tell yourself you've missed your chance or won't make it; you can do it. Being intentional with your husband does not take much time or energy. When our husbands know we love the Lord and are committed to our relationship with Jesus, we love and adore them; they feel secure and respected.

## Seeds of Communication

In my many years of mentoring young, newly married women, I share with them that *marriage is like a flower. We must water and tend to that flower, or the flower will wither up and die.* If she doesn't *marriage is like a flower. We must water and tend to that flower, or the flower will wither up and die.* water and tend to it, another woman will. It happens so often. I see couples who have been married for years and then divorced suddenly. Your husband is your sweetheart, and we must not let another woman treat him better than you do. We must be on watch and be intentional with our relationship with our husbands. The devil desires to destroy homes and lives.

Think back to why you fell in love in the first place. Something drew you two together and made you say "yes" to spending the rest of your days with him. He was your choice. Loving your husband is not always easy. When life kicks in, children arrive, or relationships get messy, we must look for the good and praise it. Scripture tells us in Psalm 120:2-4 and 126:2 that the mouth contains both words of wickedness and praise. Our tongues have the power to produce excellent and wicked fruit. The wise woman appropriately chooses her words. With her encouraging and kind words, she can contribute to spiritual health and the development of others through good medicine (Proverbs 12:18 and 16:23). Most of our disagreements with her husbands can be resolved if we speak the truth in love and realize he is not a mind reader.

Another tool I use to communicate with my husband so I am not nagging at him is my "Honey Do List." A "Honey Do List" is an ongoing list of extra things I need help with or things he needs to repair or do around the house. When he has time, he completes the task. If it is something urgent, he will help me at the moment. Over the years, we have established respect for one another and will help each other whenever and whatever is needed.

## Seeds of Constant Learning

As a mother of four sons who have lived with five males for over 25 years, I've learned that males are genuinely different from us. Their thinking, perspectives, and views often blow my mind. I recommend both if you have never looked up your husband's birth order (I'm first born married to the youngest) or took a personality test together. I am not here to down the male species. I only want to point out that they are different in every way! Their differences made us fall in love with them in the first place. When I read scripture and look in Genesis at creation, I realize how unique each of us is. Sadly, we as a woman want to transform our husbands, expecting them to communicate and react the same way a close friend would. Not to sound harsh, but your husband does not want to come home to hear about your finding hamburger meat on sale for $2.99. He loves and cares about you but could care less about things like this. Just like you (if you work outside the home), he has spent the last 8-9 hours in a competitive world that is not kind. You may have spent hours working outside the house as well. Just be mindful that men have a "nothing box." We speak of it often in our homes. They don't think about things the way women do. I encourage you to study with your husband. Learn about what kind of man he is. Learn all his favorites! Know his favorite color, candy bar, team, foods, etc. He should be not only your husband but also your best friend.

## Seeds of Never Surrendering (Without a Biblical cause)

Lest you are reading and thinking that I have a perfect marriage or that I must manipulate or control everything here at home, you are mistaken. Our 25th year of marriage was challenging. We both thought it was over and were desperate to find out how we got to where we were. Thank God for good marriage counseling and conferences. We got the help we needed. We worked hard listening to one another and created harmony in our new season of life.

Remember, nothing happens by accident. We must work to maintain the beautiful flower of our marriages for the sake of generations to come. *We must intentionally fan the embers of romance in our marriages.* We can do this by going on

*We must intentionally fan the embers of romance in our marriages.*

weekly dates (even if it's just a cup of coffee for 15 minutes to connect), praying for one another both together and separately, sending a text throughout the day to say "love you," forgiving often, listening, respecting one another, and forever being thankful that the Lord placed us together. The enemy seeks to destroy the family by creating an atmosphere of hostility. Fight back. Don't do the devil's job for him. If the devil will lie to you about how you would be better off without your husband, make him log his hours. Don't help him! Pray for your husband, especially in front of your children. Compliment him in front of others. Hold his hand in public. Wear his favorite perfume and spray a little on his pillow once a week when you change the bed sheets. Place a love note in his lunch box. Develop photos of just you two without the children and display them on the shelves of your houses, in his office, and on your car's dashboard. Leave a romantic note under his pillow or on his desk at the office. Purchase new lingerie, wrap it, and leave it at his office or workplace. And, of course, be intimate with him.

## Seeds of Intimacy

I am shocked at how many women forget their sweethearts once their children arrive. Friends, your husband desires intimacy. Some may say I am out of place saying this, but it is true! Sex is a part of God's design. Put a lock on your bedroom door and guard your alone time with your husband. Make time after a long day to talk, rub his back, and be present. Growing up, my parents would do devotions and pray with us, then we were in our rooms, and they would go into their room with the TV on and the door locked. We never questioned what they were doing. They were always appropriate. They taught us by example that their alone time to connect in marriage was meaningful. Their anniversary was in the fall, and they would take an overnight trip each year. They would arrange for me, my brother, and my younger sister to stay with family or friends. These arrangements made me feel so secure. I knew my mom and dad were committed to each other. Their relationship was solid and alone time was a priority. I have modeled and protected my marriage because of their excellent example. Before my daddy went to Heaven, they celebrated 50 years of marriage. Making time for one another is critical to a successful marriage.

When teaching piano, I tell my students, **"Practice makes permanent, not perfect!"** The same is true in the bedroom. We must practice, practice, practice! It takes hard work, and we must read books on the subject and do whatever it takes to get this right. For many, this part of being a wife is not enjoyable. I encourage you to talk with your husband about your feelings and preferences. Attend a Family Life Conference or listen to a podcast from other believers on this subject. Be proactive.

When our sons were in their teens, and life was super busy with work, ministry, or, you name it, we had to find a system that worked for us. So, I began placing a red heart 2-3 days a week. I would prepare myself throughout the day. I would empty my mind, so my focus was on him exclusively. You must mentally prepare by asking the Lord to help you stay focused on your sweetheart. This preparation is where the magic begins. It took me almost a year to figure this out. I will always be grateful for this advice as a young bride. A healthy sex life comes with so many advantages. Your heart health will benefit. You will also build your immune system and relieve stress. Do your research and plan accordingly. I promise you it gets better and better.

Making alone time a priority will make your husband feel respected and secure enough to open up and grow in your relationship. Most of our dates were around the TV in the living room when our boys went to sleep. Simple things together made us more substantial for the journey. As our sons grew and it was easier to find sitters, we would get away once a year for a few days. I realize this is not possible for everyone, but get creative. Swap sitters with a friend. Just be present and intentional in planning to be intimate with your husband each week. Even if you have to have a "staycation" where the children leave occasionally, and you have the house to yourselves, make it work. Marriage becomes much sweeter when you prioritize this and seek to be with your husband. Life will never be the same!

## Seeds of Individuality

Regarding our marriages, I believe the Lord allows us to meet and marry our opposites. At the beginning of your relationship, you may not see him as your opposite, but you live together for a few years, then add a few children. Joe and I are opposites! I am not always negative, but sometimes I see the glass as half empty. In contrast, he sees it half full and running over most of the time. The other day I was sharing unpleasant news with him, and he immediately looked at the bright side and how it could have been a simple misunderstanding or miscommunication. Before I knew it, these words jumped out of my mouth: "Just say something negative!" Oh, how I was wrong and had to apologize. That's just how Joe is - always looking for the good.

Finding the positive is a struggle, and I constantly strive to improve. While we are different in many ways, we show a shared love for our family, a strong faith, and a love for humanity. I enjoy acts of service and being around all different types of people and places. I've never met a stranger. Joe finds his joy in staying in one place, investing in the community by ministering, teaching the word, and pouring the gospel into families in our local church. Yet, we've found balance because of our differences, not despite them. You and your husband can do the same. It's ok that you have different preferences. You both grew up differently. Each of you had your family traditions and ways of doing life. Now you get to create your family legacy. Celebrate your differences, and don't try to change how God created each of you. Pray for him, specifically that he will become the husband and father the Lord made him become.

**List a few ways you and your husband can plan to be intimate today. Time will bring new possibilities to your marriage.**

*We plant, we water, we wait, and then we harvest! Water the seeds that mean the most to you!*

# Chapter 5

## Your Children – Water the Seeds of Parenting

*Tell your children of it, and let your children tell their children and their children and another generation. – Joel 1:3*

Your family legacy includes your beliefs, actions, and the guidance you demonstrate in your everyday life. These actions can have lasting and multi-generational effects on your family. Aspects that are often overlooked but remain critical in forming your family legacy include attitudes, behaviors, communication styles, and traditions. *These things help create long-lasting deposits into your child's memory bank.* Your thoughts and beliefs create your reality, so know that just because you grew up thinking a certain way or didn't have specific values, you can change the trajectory of your family and the legacy you leave.

> *These things help create long-lasting deposits into your child's memory bank.*

What you are doing inside your home will impact future generations. For our family, a tradition was born that affected our attitudes, behaviors, and communication style. After our first

Christmas, we realized that being "full-time" in ministry would not allow us to engage in special Christmas gift-giving. My husband and I decided to write one another a love letter and hang them on our Christmas tree. Every Christmas morning, we wake up to a unique letter hanging from the tree. Our children have watched us for years read, laugh, and (sometimes) weep when we read expressions of love and gratitude given through these unique love letters. Another legacy we continue to leave to our children is reading a Bible story or devotional and praying together every night before bed. Whatever you choose to do, know that children remember moments, not days.

Joe and I work hard at building our relationships with our sons. Not only as their parents who love and adore them but also as their mentors and friends now that they are older. We already shared a parent-child relationship by God's design, but that was just the beginning. Our goal has been to be long, grace-driven parents who would open and win our children's hearts. We committed to being the wisest and best companions in their lives. Remember that you are the wise one with whom you want your children to walk. They need you to be wise in how you help them navigate their relationships. I pray daily that the Lord will add His favor to my family. *Our homes are the single most powerful arena on earth.* Lives on this earth are being shaped and changed forever. It took me a few years to realize how valuable and desperately I desired to become a mother.

*Our homes are the single most powerful arena on earth.*

After being married for several years, having a family became uncertain, and I had a few medical problems that prevented me from becoming pregnant. During the last doctor's visit before becoming pregnant with our first son, the doctor shared that we would probably never have children. With much prayer and anticipation, we made the appointment to begin infertility treatments. I was teaching school, and many students were sick with the flu. The day of my appointment arrived, and I had not been feeling well but thought I was getting the flu. As a routine, the nurse asked me to take a pregnancy test. I was sick to my stomach at the thought of taking another test. However, if we were going to start infertility treatments, this had to be done. To our surprise, we were pregnant! What an answered prayer. I often want to go back and show this doctor the miracle of our four sons and how we could have a family.

But I'm not foolish to think that this is everyone's story. My heart hurts for the ladies whose outcome was not like mine. For those with children, whether by birth, adoption, or foster care, we must prioritize teaching them about Jesus - that he is their best friend. Proverbs 13:22 says a good man/woman leaveth an inheritance for his children's children. Inheritance is more than material wealth. Our heritage includes the legacy we pass on to the next generation. We must model for our children how to focus on Jesus and never forget that He is with them and has a beautiful plan for their lives no matter the circumstances they face in life. As mothers, we must proclaim His presence to our children because the lost world is watching.

## Seeds of Expectations

When raising our boys, we shared that people judge them by three things: 1. How we talk. 2. Our appearance, and 3. Our actions. Each day we would "practice" how we spoke to one another, take pride in our clothing, and work fervently on actions. We would practice good manners by role-playing and exposing them to different situations. Children learn by doing, so modeling behaviors create an atmosphere of trust. Children also need structure, routine, consistency, and reliability. By being intentional every day and practicing our words, tones, and body language, they learn by example how to behave.

So often, our homes become hotels. We sleep there. Don't allow your home to become a hotel. Research tells us that children's personalities, behaviors, and brain development are profoundly impacted by age three. The most rapid period of growth for the human brain is in the earliest years of life. We must not forget to be intentional with the little ones entrusted to our care. Establish daily routines with your child, so they will anticipate what and when things happen. Teach them that interrupting when two adults are talking is rude. However, teach them to gently squeeze your hand or arm if it is important or an emergency. I would gladly stop my conversation and address what was needed when this happened. This one action helped our boys know that Mom was always available.

Read a special book at the end of the day, and say your prayers every night. Get to know your child's favorite color, candy, food, Bible story, etc. Create daily habits that will enhance their little minds to know Jesus through the routines we establish.

## Seeds of Preparation

Talk to your children and teach them. Then model how they are to include and interact with those children and adults with special needs, individuals of different backgrounds and cultures, homeless people, and strangers. Train them that if someone picks them up to abduct them, to scream, "You are not my mom" or "You are not my dad." These words will alert those around them that they are not just throwing a fit. Train them to be aware of their surroundings and to always travel in a buddy system. We taught our sons that there is power in numbers. Stick with a buddy at all times. Also, train them to locate a mother with a child if they get separated or lost from you in the store or another venue. She will be more likely to help them get the assistance they need to find you. Mothers with children are usually safe people to be a helper.

Read Bible stories, pray, sing songs, memorize Bible verses, and model kindness. Make a list or write songs or hymns in your calendar to teach your child. Make it an appointment and keep it. If teaching something new each week overwhelms you, do it monthly, which would only be twelve verses or songs. It doesn't take hours upon hours to teach children new things. A few moments a day singing a new song or learning a Bible verse will be life-altering.

Each of our sons entered the world hearing their daddy singing his favorite hymn, "Blessed Assurance." He sang it to them almost daily when they were babies, and as they grew up, they were taught the words and meanings. Teaching children about Jesus doesn't have to happen in big, grand gestures. Often it is in daily interactions that our faith is building. *Children don't remember days; they remember moments.* Their character is transformed into one small interaction or conversation at a time. Take time to plan opportunities to shape your child's character. Repeat these lessons often. The pattern of repetition will be planted in their little minds, and you will one day see results. Our children's character tomorrow is shaped by what we teach them today.

## Seeds of Excellence

From my observations, raising boys is so much different from girls. Boys sometimes have difficulty expressing feelings or keeping their temper in check. At our house, we always say, "I love you." Some people grow up never hearing their parents say, "I love you." I was not one of these. Love flowed freely in my home. We made it a point to say it often. However, on hard days when they did not feel like talking, or the environment called for silence, I taught our sons to tap on my arm three times: I love you! I would then tap it back. We have used this especially as they got older and were in places where they needed to hear it, but we could not vocalize it.

Another phrase we would post around the house and make bookmarks of was "Take the High Road." "Taking the High Road" means choosing between the better and the best. There are so many decisions to be made during the day, and we wanted our sons to think about their choices and behaviors. We would practice behaviors at home each week for when we went out in public. When we mastered new skills and chores were completed each week, we rewarded them Friday night with a "Pallot Night." Pallot Night consisted of sleeping in the living room, playing a board game, watching a movie, and eating homemade pizza. "Pallot Night" was an event they looked forward to even as teenagers. The memories of bonding and building friendships were well worth all the pizza and games in the world. This one small, planned intention continues in our adult children's conversations and memories every time we get together.

## Seeds of Planning

Planning and being intentional in your child's life each day is necessary for learning to take place. It is never about micro-managing or controlling everything; it is about being intentional in what we teach and how we train our children. I kept a daytimer with a running list of things I wanted to teach them.

One of these lessons was teaching our children how to sit at restaurants. We practiced this at home. We sat at the table every night for dinner. When an occasion arrived, and we went to a restaurant, we pretended we were already there. We role-played how to lay napkins in laps, use manners, etc. The same was practiced for church services. We would "pretend" church by playing a tape of Charles Stanley or Adrian Rodgers. Our boys could not get up from the couch until their sermon was complete. I would sit with them. I gave them a notebook and crayons, and they could draw anything. However, they could not get up or talk to the bathroom. We also practiced being reverent. I then took those same notebooks and crayons to an actual church service. The boys would take a potty break between Sunday school and big church. Their behavior was not always perfect, but with children, more is caught than taught, And our children knew our expectations.

Children have a higher chance of meeting those expectations when we talk to them and share the expectations for behavior. Depending on the age, we must practice, talk, practice, talk, practice, and talk and practice some more. Repetition is the key. In these moments, we are teaching our children how to behave. Consistency is the key. You are leading them by example to sit at the table with manners at home and in a restaurant. You also teach them to sit in church.

We also practice at home how we act in the library, the grocery store, etc., before going. Little people are a joy to be around. They are bright, teachable, and honest. They live for boundaries. They want to structure with a schedule. They desire routine with security. When we are intentional with our children, they will grow up feeling loved and secure.

## Seeds of Working Hard

As children grow, teach them the value of hard work and grit. Give them a daily chore and teach them that they are part of a team- the family. Working together in keeping the house clean and in order, as well as yard work and other necessities, prepares them for adulthood. At ten years old, our boys began doing their laundry. If you are not ready to share this chore, allow them to hang up items, iron, or do other tasks. Please encourage them by sharing that they will grow up and become productive citizens. Trust me, positive words that echo throughout your home will be living testimonies in the days ahead.

## Seeds of Safety

When children are young and begin vocalizing their feelings, it is important to model appropriate behaviors. We want them to feel safe and know God is always with them. We did this by forming a "family password" in case of an emergency. If someone were to pick them up instead of me or Dad, that trusted adult would have to know this password. If someone was to pick our boys up from sports, school, church, etc. and did not have the password, they were NOT to go with them. Since we only have one son at home (the others are all adults), I can share our password: "Peanut Butter Pizza."

We recently had a situation where we had to leave my son's phone in the school office for him to pick up after we had it repaired. I texted him toward the end of the school day to see if he had retrieved his phone. The return text was very vague. I became concerned that someone had taken his phone. When I asked if this was my son, he sent the words "Peanut Butter Pizza." I knew it was him. What a joy it is to have connections with your children.

## Seeds of Example

When we put feelings into words, children feel safe and secure. Self-regulation often occurs in this safety and security, and children can learn to manage their emotions and fears. Model for your child how to use words to express wants and needs. For example, if another sibling or child tries to take a toy from them, instead of whining or crying, teach them to say, "I had it first; chose something else." Our famous saying in the Storey home is, "Be nice or be quiet."

Words are powerful. As they grew older, we often said, "You can be mad, but you cannot be mean to one another." I am not naïve enough to think our sons never fussed or fought. If they did, Mom didn't see it. They knew the house rule was to be respectful and that "things that are different are not the same." Meaning that they are different. God made them different. It's ok that they don't all like the same things or even think the same ways. Individuality is how we raised them: to love Jesus and to be independent thinkers, to stand firm for their beliefs, and to be passionate about what the Lord has placed in their hearts to do.

In respecting one another and the roles God designed for us in Ephesians 6:1-4, I also taught our sons that their daddy "hung the moon and made chocolate." Not really, but close. Even on days when I wanted to hide their daddy's body in my trunk and then help people look for him, I never spoke a negative word about him. When we degrade or say degrading towards their daddy, it harms their development. Tell them you love and appreciate Dad's hard work for the family. Even if their dad does not give 100%, he will feel appreciated once he hears his children are his fans.

## Seeds of Connection

Another way I stay connected with our children as they grow into young men is to text every morning. I usually share a scripture or a meme that will carry them throughout the day. Sometimes when I text "love you," my autocorrect will change it to "live." I've thought about this often. To love is to live, and we must live to love. Our children feel loved when we provide space for them to feel secure. Always tell them the truth and keep your promises. What you say is what you will do. Be reliable and available to them. When teaching reliability, let them know you will always be here for them, but most importantly, God is always with them. Get a day planner and intentionally spend time with each child alone for 30 minutes. Find out their favorite color, candy bar, or movie; make a list with them about every place or everything they want to do in their life before going to Heaven. Have a special song that you share that is only yours together. If you're a boy mom, dance to it at his wedding. I've done this twice and preparing for the third time next summer.

Know your children. Have boundaries, but cultivate a friendship as they grow older. You will reap the benefits through a harvest of conversations and develop a close-knit relationship as they launch into adulthood. Our children's character tomorrow is shaped by what we teach them today.

## Seeds of Letting Go

Deuteronomy 6:7 reminds us to teach our children diligently. *The days are long, but the years are short.* Enjoy your journey with your precious gift(s)

> *The days are long, but the years are short.*

from Heaven. I know the days are exhausting, but there will be a day when you will wake up, and they will be blasting off into adulthood. It's the way the Lord intended for it to be. Yes, it's a little sad. But super rewarding when you've been intentional in building a life-lasting relationship.

Imagine if you live each day intentionally. You will have little or no regrets. Get better every day, pouring into the lives of your children. Pray daily for your children. I pray these prayers every morning for our sons: I pray they will

- Know Christ as their Savior early in life.

- Have a hatred for sin and be caught when guilty.

- Be protected from evil in all areas of life: spiritual, mental, emotional, and physical.

- Have a responsible attitude as they grow in their relationships with others.

- Respect those in authority and have the desire to make and keep the right kinds of friends as He protects them from the wrong type of friends.

- Be kept from the wrong mate and saved for the right one.

- Be totally submitted to the call of God in their lives and actively resist Satan in all circumstances.

Finally, I pray the Lord will put a hedge of protection around them so they cannot find their way to the wrong people or places and the wrong people cannot find their way to them. Pray for and discuss their temperaments, including self-control, politeness, good manners, and a happy attitude. Pray for whom they will grow up and marry. Pray aloud for their struggles in math or with a bully. Pray they will easily make friends. Ask daily for answered prayers and praise the Lord together for His answering. Leave a legacy of faith and love for the next generation to discuss.

Recently, something I had planned and a direction I believed the Lord wanted me to go in was altered. Because I had left a full-time career and chose only to teach part-time, an opportunity I interviewed for chose a candidate who did not pause their career. My plans were no longer valid. What I believed to be the Lord's will became a "no." For a moment, I gave the devil space in my head. I felt like a failure. Thoughts of not being good enough began sneaking in. As the sun filled the bedroom window one day, I realized that my priorities and investments in our family were never about a position or a paycheck. It hit me like a ton of bricks. That morning, each of our sons was on their rocket ship headed to the moon! One was in Corpus Christi, Texas, deep sea fishing; another in New Orleans, Louisiana, marking off a "bucket list" dream; another hiking the Appalachian Mountains near North Carolina (something he has wanted to do since he was a small boy); and our youngest was in the next room singing worship songs as he played guitar and gave thanks for several college scholarships offers.

All my long days of intentions, routines, read-aloud, fort building, bike rides, hikes, taxi rides, etc., were not in vain. I lived intentionally while raising our sons. I placed daily deposits into our sons' daily memory banks. Perfect life? No! I've dealt with a son's diagnosis of an auto-immune disease, mental illness, the suicide of a close teen friend of my sons, and broken hearts from young love - all a part of a sin-filled world.

Our children are valuable and dear to our hearts. I have, planted seeds of adventure and self-worth; watered and watered and watered and watered; dove deep into the Word; prayed over, prayed for, and fast; and now I am beginning to reap the harvest. Don't give up! Your harvest day is fast approaching!

**What do you want your children to remember most about their childhood?**

*We plant, we water, we wait, and then we harvest! Water the seeds that mean the most to you!*

# Chapter 6
## Your Community – Water the Seeds of Friendship

*A friend loves at all times. – Proverbs 17:17 ESV*

Community is a lifestyle with a common purpose: connecting with others and their walk with Jesus. Phillippians 2:1:2 reminds us that if there is any encouragement in Christ, any comfort from love, any participation in the Spirit, any affection and sympathy, complete with joy by agreeing, having the same love, being in full accord and of one mind.

Understanding that many women are "hungry" for human connections provides many opportunities to shine brightly. Often they bless many with our testimonies of His goodness. We each have 24 hours a day. We are asleep at seven-eight hours, and then we work (either at home with children, home educating, or out in the workforce). Then, we spend about one hour reading our Bible, praying, practicing self-care, etc. - caring for ourselves as a "whole woman." All the other hours could be planned to be a blessing to others.

As Christian women, our lives are not divided into separate parts. We are Christians 100% all the time. So, evaluate the ways you connect to your community. It is more than church attendance or dropping money into the Salvation Army Bucket during the holidays. *You cannot impact the people in your community unless they know you exist.* Consider these ideas when reaching out to your community:

*You cannot impact the people in your community unless they know you exist.*

- Bring another mom into your home and allow her to observe you cooking a meal, folding clothes, and interacting with your children.

- Quietly say a blessing over your lunch at work.

- Volunteer in the nursery at church, the Children's Ministry, a food pantry, a nursing facility, your child's school, etc.

- Give treat bags to the individuals who pick up your trash each week.

- Leave an extra tip at a restaurant with an encouraging "Pass-It-On" card.

- Ask the grocery store's cashier about their favorite candy bar. Purchase it, and before you exit the store, give it to them with an encouraging "you are doing a great job" or whatever the Holy Spirit leads.

Community is important and instrumental in encouraging women to be their best selves. When we share stories of our lives to enhance the development of another woman's journey, we provide her with a great sense of self-worth and dignity. The community also promotes support systems that, in turn, encourage resilience and new opportunities to learn and unlearn actions that will inspire and help others. A great sense of empowerment can be created when we allow ourselves to be open and vulnerable to grow in God-given relationships. This empowerment gives women a voice in culture, media, and even churches to make a difference in the lives of others.

## Seeds of Friendships

Finding other ladies in the same season of life and asking them to join you on the journey will enhance your spiritual growth. We call these relationships/ friendships "Accountability Partners" in our home. For me, it has one or two individuals who are on your child's pickup list or emergency list - ones you could call in the middle of the night to help you with your children or the ones you call to ask for a casserole when you are too sick to cook for your family.

An accountability partner is a close friend who prays with you and for you. This person is one you trust and can be transparent with and one from whom you can accept their truth in love. Another way accountability partners work is to have a friend you reach out to weekly (or daily), asking if she is reading her Bible, praying, thinking good thoughts, and guarding her eyes and ears. These partners can be formed from anywhere in your community but are often created within the walls of your church. Remember that attending church won't get you to Heaven, but it will create a sense of belonging.

## Seeds of Belonging

*The community can also provide a great sense of self-worth and dignity to a weary soul.*

*The community can also provide a great sense of self-worth and dignity to a weary soul.* Often just being around Christians

69

can reduce anxiety and depression. When we feel included in something bigger than ourselves, we can cope with life's happenings and seasons. We can even relieve the tensions and stresses the world piles on us. Community gives us strength through the support we feel from others. We can also share our wisdom, encouraging others to make it through another day. Other ways to encourage others to feel like they belong are to send a note, text, call, etc. Hebrews 3:13 says to encourage one another daily as long as it is called today. When someone comes to mind, act on it.

## Seeds of Trust

People are naturally inclined not to trust one another. Untrust makes it hard for women to interact with modern society. Developing trusting relationships will connect women and add value to life. Sharing and accepting women where they are is also important because we are all in different seasons of life. The community also encourages us to give and volunteer our time and talents to other women freely and without judgment. Social connections dramatically influence our spiritual life; how we feel and see situations daily will also build trust. These relationships will keep us going throughout the days, weeks, months, and years ahead of us.

The Bible is filled with examples of people who ministered in the community. The Lord loves people. He died for us and has a plan for our lives. The prophet Jeremiah shares that before we were even born, He knew us (Jeremiah 1:5). Psalm 139:13 explains that we are important enough for God to know us and to be involved in who we are and what we are becoming. What is it that He is calling you to do in your community? Will you listen to His voice as you read the pages of this book? Will you say "yes" to the amazing life He has purposed for you as you shine brightly in your community?

# Seeds of Saying "Yes"

Think of all the ordinary individuals God used throughout the Bible: Noah, Paul, David, John, Mary, and Jesus. What if Noah had said, "I don't do animals or mess with boats?" What if the Apostle Paul had said, "God, I don't write well?" We would not have the majority of the New Testament. What if little David had said, "God, I don't handle giants well," or John the Baptist had said, "I am not sure I can baptize anyone." What if Mary said, "God, I don't believe in a virgin birth." Instead, she said, "Here am I." Imagine if Jesus said, "God, I don't do crosses." Praise the Lord; Jesus died for our sins and rose for our salvation! How will you impact your community for Christ? Remember, more opportunities are ahead as long as you are still here!

**List two ways you can connect in your community this week:**

*We plant, we water, we wait, and then we harvest. Water the seeds that matter the most to you!*

# Chapter 7
## Your Dwelling – Water the Seeds of Home Management

*The wise woman buildeth her house, but the foolish plucketh it down with her hands. – Proverbs 14:1*

How can you manage your day? You really can't. The Earth is spinning 16,000 miles per hour, 24 hours a day, with 1440 minutes and 86,400 seconds daily. There is nothing we can do to change this. You can manage yourself, your behaviors, your choices, and your time. Make it count.

Managing your home schedule is vital in every family, contributing to overall health, happiness, and well-being. Working the home involves planning the home environment (routines, menus, bedtimes, etc.). The concept of organization is the planning executed by those management skills. As disturbing as this is, you can ask my family what I want on my tombstone, and without hesitation, they will tell you: "Everything has a home!" This statement has been spoken from my lips thousands of times throughout my life. When a home has everything in its place and a place for everything, half the battle of managing a home is won.

## Seeds of Administration

Being intentional inside our homes requires daily planning and action. The word intentionality means showing up for what I hoped to be true. As I mentioned in a previous chapter, I plan on Sunday afternoons. My week is already scheduled when I fall asleep on Sunday night, and intentions are in place. Are the plans I make flexible? Yes. Were there daily reminders that the Storey Household is a team? Absolutely! However, the daily seeds of routines I intentionally planted in our children's hearts and minds are non-negotiable.

One habit I started as a teenager and have been passed down to our sons is morning devotions. When our sons were at home, we had a "rule": "No Bible, no breakfast." Each son would come to breakfast after quiet prayer and reading Proverbs. Breakfast after Bible time was not legalistic or harsh; spending time with Jesus before breakfast was a habit. This habit helped me encourage good habits and manage our crazy morning schedules. This example is just the beginning of home management and organization with children. You already have patterns that are either growing those you love into independent humans or making you dread every morning.

## Seeds of Direction

Every woman has a system for running her household. I am not reinventing the wheel. Instead, I encourage you to plan your days and work out your plan. Set weekly cleaning chores. Make menus (Meatloaf Mondays, Taco Tuesdays, etc.), a laundry schedule, a grocery list, etc., and stick to them. All this planning will give you more hours in your days. If you do not have a system, use the ones on my website to get started. Sometimes *we must imitate before we innovate.* Maybe you

*we must imitate before we innovate.*

did not grow up in a calm, clutter-free atmosphere, or perhaps you are like me some days, climbing out from under the piles. Either way, initially, I found how I wanted to run our home, imitated what I learned, then innovated ways that worked well for a family.

A technique that has aided my time management is the Pomodoro system. Then-university student Francesco Cirillo developed the Pomodoro Technique in 1980. Cirillo struggled to stay focused and finish his assignments. Feeling overwhelmed, he committed ten minutes a day to study. He found a tomato (Pomodoro in Italian) shaped egg timer, and the Pomodoro technique was born. He wrote a book about his methods, but the short version is as follows:

- Get a to-do list and timer.
- Set the timer for 25 minutes and focus till it sounds.
- Take a 5-minute break and begin again.

Procrastination has little to do with laziness or lack of self-control. Instead, staring down a big task, project, to-do list, etc., is uncomfortable, so we avoid it altogether. We may turn on a TV program or social media to boost our mood. Defeating procrastination is precisely what the Pomodoro technique asks you to do. Once you start whatever you are doing for 5+ minutes, add minutes, and the hyper-focus on one thing will allow success to follow—one step at a time. Whether exercising, cleaning a closet, or organizing a drawer, this technique will help you get motivated. Please make a list and print it out (or download mine free on my website and imitate until you innovate). Have this in front of you daily so your intentions don't get kicked out the door when life kicks in.

Since I hate cleaning the house and we don't have extra money for a house cleaner each week, I divide and conquer a little bit every day. Many of you work full-time outside the home, and many of you with young children work full-time inside the house. To eliminate cleaning all day on Saturdays, I sweep and mop our hardwood floors and clean the kitchen before bed. I divide the other cleaning chores from Monday-Thursdays. For example, on Mondays, I clean all the bathrooms, mirrors, and windows. On Tuesdays, I change the bed sheets and vacuum the house. I also do laundry. On Wednesdays, I wipe down the doors, walls, and baseboards; I do a few loads of laundry too! On Thursdays, I clean the bathrooms and mirrors again and finish laundry for the week. Completing a few jobs each day may seem like a lot, but I set a timer for 10 minutes at a time and get this done in about 20 minutes or less. Staying ultra-focused on these things adds up to a clean house. I always keep the living room and kitchen presentable because of the company that drops in or the friends who come home with the boys. This eliminates any stress I have for visitors.

Many hands make for light work. If you don't have a system, create your own, but be kind to yourself. Divide out the garbage chore, pet feeding, dishwasher unloading, sweeping, etc., to the "Family Team" that lives there.

## Seeds of Routine

One piano piece was challenging for me when I was young and taking piano lessons. I was to play it in the winter recital. I complained about how it was "too hard" and how I could not possibly learn it all. Daddy asked me, "Sonya, how do you eat an elephant?" I sarcastically responded, "I don't know… how do you eat an elephant?" He smiled and said, "One bite at a time." At this point, I could not care less about eating elephants—I wanted an easier piece to play in the recital and became agitated.

My dad was an amazing pastor, leader, and friend. He and my mom both invested in people. They both set monthly and yearly goals and worked toward success. They encouraged me to do the same. Their care and intentional upbringing have made all the difference in my life. Their daily routines and rhythms taught me, my brother, and my sister, how to live. Once these habits set in, a lifestyle of success followed my parents throughout their ministry. Now, as adults, my siblings and I continue sowing the seeds we learned when we were younger. We are all reaping a harvest now. For years I have passed on this method to our sons, and as a result, each has a plan of action for their dreams and desires. Did this happen overnight? No, it happened one day at a time; what you do today matters.

## Seeds of Overseeing Daily Operations

Sometimes we neglect to care for our homes until things get out of hand or in a painful mess. I once heard a story of a farmer who walks up to find an older man sitting in a rocking chair. Next to him was his old dog. The dog is moaning and groaning. The farmer asked the old man, "Why is your dog moaning and groaning?" The older man replied, "Because he is sitting on a nail." The farmer asked, "Why doesn't he move?" The older man said, "Because it is not hurting him enough to move." Not taking action or changing behavior is how most of us (women, wives, moms, sisters, friends) operate.

We complain about our lack of organization, control, or freedom, yet in the same breath, we discount the values of organizational systems, habits, or a well-designed routine. Freedom requires routines and structure. Routine and structure make freedom possible. Routines and structure liberate creativity. Routines align with freedom and allow freedom to flourish. Freedom without structure and routine is chaos. However, freedom in our homes can reign with the right systems and routines. So, to operate a home where peace is a priority and your home becomes a safe, simple, clear, and safe haven (a little bit of Heaven on earth) specific process is how it's accomplished. I pray after reading this book that you will create rhythms that help your house to become a "home," a safe shelter from the world's chaos.

One process is to create a daily routine for your family that is simple and clear. This process will leave everyone free to fly and become everything the Lord intended for them to be. *Creativity thrives on routine.* I have experienced this in my own *Creativity thrives on routine.* life and our sons' lives. We have four of the most creative young men I have ever been around. Having a daily routine enhanced these desires for creativity and ingenuity. Being intentional about our daily routines enhances creativity and innovation. It touches not only your life but the lives around you. We are today what we are becoming! After reading this chapter and thinking about your daily routines, "What are you becoming?"

**What two routines do you want to begin today that will enhance the legacy you are already leaving?**

*We plant, we water, we wait, and then we harvest! Water the seeds that mean the most to you!*

# Chapter 8

## Your Abundance – Water the Seeds of Generosity

*Do nothing from selfish ambition or conceit, but in humility count others more significant than yourself. – Philippians 2:3 ESV*

The word abundance means to have a large quantity of something. Having a mindset of abundance means being thankful for what you have. Seeing the bounty in our lives - whether it is time, resources, or kind words - abundant living manifests itself through our generosity. We do not give to get, but scripture is clear that God loves a cheerful giver! (2 Corinthians 9:7)

True abundance is more than possessions, money, or quantifiable things. Many people have a lot of money and success yet still lack true happiness. When we live in abundance, we can give more attention, love, and support. *Practice generosity. If you do not develop generosity, you cannot produce it.* When I think less about myself and

> *Practice generosity. If you do not develop generosity, you cannot produce it.*

more about others, life improves immensely. I become anxious when I think about my circumstances or other situations beyond my control. My focus turns toward fear. Gratitude and generosity are the antidotes to anxiety.

Consider this: Your Father is the King of the Universe, who controls the events of eternity and wants to work in your life. I had this thought back in the late 1990s when we started our family and again in 2021 when I was with my precious daddy moments before he entered the gates of Heaven: The older I get, the more I ponder my life and ask myself, "What will I do with the time I have left?" Psalms 90:12 tells us to number our days so we may apply our hearts toward wisdom. We are living on earth at this time or such a time as this (Esther 4:14). I won't be here forever, and neither will you. How we live our days, particularly how generously we live, is how those we love will remember us. We will never know the power of a generous heart on this side of Heaven.

## Seeds of Choices

I remember a story a youth pastor shared when I was 14. He compared my life to a basketball game. He said to imagine our team was down by two points and I was fouled. I had a chance to tie the game or even win it. While at the foul line, I carefully shot the basketball and missed. Game over. No win. He reminded me that life is like this. We get one shot to make our mark. I can't tell the referee, "Hey, my feet were not lined up correctly, or may I take the shot again?". Nope, once it's over, it's over. Yes, God allows us to mess up and get back up again, but that is not the point of this story. The point of this illustration is that we all have one life to live. We are in charge of the choices we make.

The secret to living is giving to others. The more generous we are in our possessions, the more is given to us. In Luke 6:38, Jesus tells us to give, and it will be given to us. Generosity is evident throughout the Bible. The quality of being kind and generous is not limited to money. The Bible is clear that we are to tithe 10% and give an offering to the church (Malachi 3:10). God doesn't need our 10% to do His work; He wants our obedience. He wants us to trust Him. When teaching tithing to our children, we asked how they would feel if the Lord asked up to keep 10% and give him 90%. Those were interesting conversations. When the Bible speaks of tithing, it is more than our money. Let us also tithe on our time. We have 24 hours in a day, so let's consider spending 2.4 hours with Jesus and pointing and pouring the love of Christ into others.

## Seeds of Giving

Years ago, a pastor shared this illustration about tithing, which altered my thought about giving. He said he was going away on a journey for several months and asked three of his buddies to help funnel resources through them to his wife and wanted to bless them in the process. He set up a system for them to give her monthly money, ensuring she was cared for. He gave each of them $10,000 a month and asked them to give his wife 10%; they could keep the rest. After a few months, he called to see how they were giving to her. The first gentleman gave the $1000 to the wife. That was the 10% requested of him. The second said he was led to give her $2000 a month just in case she had unexpected expenses. The third gentleman said he gave her $700 but had used the remaining for his family's needs. The husband was not upset with the third gentleman but made some adjustments in the months ahead. The next sentences need to be connected to this paragraph, but my computer will not allow me to connect them--The first man continued receiving the same amount because of his faithfulness. The second gentleman received $15,000 and was told to keep the remaining because he faithfully looked out for his bride. The third gentleman was cut off because he previously didn't care about his bride. This husband gave his money to take care of his wife. It was personal to him. Tithing is personal. Scripture tells us that the Church is the Bride of Christ. When we give our tithes and offerings, God blesses our lives. We do not give to get, but again, the more we give to others, the more God blesses our lives.

Money and wealth are not wrong. God is the maker and giver of wealth (Deuteronomy 8:18). Often, God allows those who excel in using their talents and abilities for the Lord to increase in material and spiritual riches (Proverbs 22:4). God does not condemn those who acquire wealth, but encourages them to use it as a means to an end, which is to glorify God (Proverbs 15:16, I Corinthians 10:31 and 2 Corinthians. 9). The scriptures recount numerous occasions when people of wealth and substance used their money to help others in need (Proverbs 14:21, Galatians 2:10), to encourage the work of the gospel (Phil. 4:15-16 and I Tim. 5:17-18), and to carry the burden of their families so others wouldn't have to accept responsibility (I Timothy 5:9).

God says that the love of money and material goods is wrong; this attitude is the root of evil (I Timothy 6:10). Again, money is not the only way to be generous. We can be helpful by donating to a local food bank, purchasing extra school supplies for a teacher, collecting extra toiletries for a homeless shelter, or purchasing extra pet food for the animal shelter. Whatever it is, your husband, children, and friends should be a part of your generosity. Again, more is caught than taught. The little people in your care will become adults living as you've modeled for them. Take them to pick an Angel from the Angel Tree at Christmas, ship a shoebox during Christmas with Operation Christmas Child, take "artwork" to a nursing home for the resident's rooms, bake a pie for a neighbor, or buy a friend an ice cream at school. Whatever it is, teach them generosity. I will never forget a co-worker buying me a Coca-Cola during a long training. It was such a small gesture. Twenty years later, I remember it being one of the kindest things that happened to me as an adult. This one act of kindness sparked a friendship that continues today.

## Seed of Example

Your friends, the people you care for and minister to, look at your life, often following your example. I know it is a lot on our shoulders. He is strengthening you with every seed of generosity you plant. Instead of thinking you "have to do this," realize you "get to do this" and be a blessing to others. Maya Angelou reminds us, "Your legacy is every life you've touched."

What kind of legacy do you want to leave? At the end of my days, I want people to cry at my funeral. I want them to remember me as a generous, kind, Jesus-loving person who was always thinking about the needs of others. Maybe this is not important to you. Perhaps you've never thought about this before. If people don't like you, they won't like our God. I don't mean to sound like a Pollyanna who wants to make others feel inadequate in comparison, but I was hoping you could consider our influence in the world and on everyone who interacts with us daily. To quote Jesus from The Chosen movie series, "There are times to stir the water" (which means we need to sometimes make a little trouble by speaking the truth in love) and stand firm for our beliefs. However, we should also vocalize these hard things without compromising who we are. Think of it this way: People are one person from a different life. Let me explain. I have spoken life into others for years by sharing that they are one decision from a totally different life. The decision could be changing one thing in their daily routine, learning a new mindset, or taking a risk on a dream the Lord placed in their heart. What I mean by one person from a totally different life is that you could be someone's difference maker. God created all of us for a purpose, and sad to say, most are not living in the potential of His calling.

Through simple encouragement, we could be the person who helps others carry on, take risks, and live the full life He has for them. Words are powerful, so we should choose them carefully and be liberal in speaking life to everyone we encounter. Also, be a servant. Servants always start the miracle. I love reading the scriptures and seeing Jesus in action. There are 37 recorded miracles that Jesus performed in the Bible. One of my favorites is the feeding of the 5.000 (Matthew 14:13-21, Mark 6:30, and Luke 9:10-17).

I look at life differently when I read stories like this one. I immediately think about this little boy's mother when I read this story. Can you imagine how she must have raised him to be generous and to have faith that his meager lunch could feed so many? What kind of mother she had to be to present an amazing son with a compassionate heart! Mothers, your training and teaching your precious little ones inside your home each day is vital! Imagine how this mother felt knowing her influence on her child changed everything that day. Thousands of people gathered in a remote place where Jesus taught and healed. Scripture says there were 5000 men plus the woman and children. When it came time for the evening meal, there was nothing for the people to eat. The Bible says that the generosity of one little boy sharing his lunch, which consisted of five small loaves of bread and two fish, made it possible to feed all of them. Jesus took the gift, thanked God for it, and used it to feed the people. He miraculously multiplied the quantity of food so that everyone was fed, and there were twelve baskets of leftovers. I like to think there was a basket for each disciple to take home as a reminder of Jesus' provision. Never forget that everything changes when we place it in Jesus' hands.

## Seeds of Extra Mile

A favorite movie in our house is the cartoon Robots featuring Robin Williams. If you have not seen it, please do so ASAP, especially with your children. Bigweld tells his friend to look around for a need and think of ideas to fill that need. We can benefit from his advice: "See a need, fill a need." Your generosity of generosity to the church and others makes a difference! Set your budget, including your generosity, and live by it. Mother Teresa said, "If you can't feed 100 people, then feed just 1." Do something! Proverbs 13:7 says, "A man (or woman) is rich according to what he is, not according to what he has." *Go the extra mile; it's never crowded!* Hold lightly to the things of this world and begin living generously every day until no breath is left in your body. Heaven depends on you to shine brightly!

> *Go the extra mile; it's never crowded!*

In all my years of ministry, I have never seen a U-Haul truck following a hearse after a funeral. We can't take stuff with us to Heaven! The person who replaces God with material things or money will be filled with grief and sorrow. Peace only comes from holding everything you have with an open hand and giving all to Him to use for His glory. Knowing and living righteously is far more important than the diligent quest for riches. Salvation provides a person with eternal benefits and rewards (Matthew 6:25-33 and Phil. 4:19).

This spiritual workout of generosity is one of the most difficult to master. Controlling your emotions, passions, and wallet takes much discipline. Proverbs continually emphasize that a person who controls their inner spirit lives prudently or in a way that shows care of thought for the future. In contrast, a foolish person allows their soul's sinful passions to dictate their path. Solomon, in the Old Testament, wrote that a person who rules their own heart is even more gallant and brave than those who conquer great cities and land (Proverb 16:32). In God's eyes, the person who is generous in their passions in giving to His kingdom is more glorious than any soldier or conqueror of the world.

What will you do with the time you have left? Do you love Jesus more than your precious possessions? Do you love Him first? Second? Third? Be assured that if you walk daily with Him, He will never fail you!

**List one area today where you will begin being generous:**

*We plant, we water, we wait, and then we harvest! Water the seeds that mean the most to you!*

# Chapter 9

Designed to be Deliberate! – Water the Seeds of
Your One Life

*Making the best use of the time because the days are evil. – Ephesians
5:16 ESV*

I believe you are reading this book to take stock of your life,
asking God for more - more to be done for Him and more to be
done through you. God's desire is for you to grab hold of a greater
vision for your life, to be more fruitful, and to take more chances
when opportunities arise. Being deliberate will enhance the life
you have been given! Consider reading a new book, author, or
genre. Perhaps you don't like football or Christian rap music, but
exposure to them won't hurt. Doing this could make a difference
in connecting you to people or your destiny. Go places you haven't
gone before, open your eyes, and see what is around you. Then,
when God opens a door of opportunity, you won't need to pray
about it or "get ready for it"; you will be ready. Doing these types
of things is what I mean by living deliberately.

A few years ago, one of my student's mothers only had a few

days to live. Her cancer had returned, and the stage four diagnosis was a blow to her entire family. This precious lady was not a Jesus follower. Her children desperately wanted to share their faith and asked me to visit with them before her passing. I was scared—but available. I made the visit afraid! I was deliberate! I remember walking into this sweet home with her three children and husband by her side. She was very ill but more than ready to accept Jesus. In her quiet voice, she prayed and asked Jesus to be her Savior. It was beautiful! Three days later, she entered Heaven. My husband, Joe, conducted the funeral, and I sang and played the piano. The peace on her children's and husband's faces is a sight I will remember forever. It was my destiny to lead this lady to Jesus. *Destiny is not a mystery; it is one deliberate decision.* Today you may be one conscious decision away from a different life.

*Destiny is not a mystery; it is one deliberate decision.*

## Seeds of Decision

When I was seven years old, I accepted Jesus as my Savior. As a child, I grew in my faith. However, it was not until I was 14 at a church camp that I dedicated my entire life to making a difference with the one life He gave me. Since that moment, as morbid as it may seem, I wake up with the thought and intent that this could be my last day on earth. My planning, decisions, and actions rest in this one thought. Am I perfect? No. Do I fail every day and have to ask for forgiveness from others? Yes, quite often. However, living with this intention is my goal. God can use one available person to change nations, communities, and the trajectory of other people's lives. One example in scripture is Abraham. In Genesis chapter 12, the Lord called Abraham to a land he would show him: no plans, no land, no job, nothing. I am confident his sweet wife Sara had questions, but she followed what the Lord had placed in her husband's heart. Our corporate "yes" changes the world.

Scripture says that He chose us before the foundation of the world. Now you may say, "I am just a stay-at-home mom." I tell you are a world changer! You say, "I am just a barista." Your coffee keeps us alive! Seriously though, God doesn't use perfect people because perfect people do not exist. We think He does, but He uses us since He does not have perfect people. My daddy, who was my pastor for years, used to say in his messages: "God doesn't call the qualified; he qualifies the called." And I add, *"If God calls you, no one in this generation can cancel you."* I am invincible until He is finished with my life. Being invincible doesn't mean I can go and play in traffic and not be taken to glory, but He will protect me in my calling. The will of God will never call you where the grace of God will not keep you.

*"If God calls you, no one in this generation can cancel you."*

## Seeds of Dreams

God uses His word to speak to us. If God has placed a dream or call in your heart, do not wait a moment to say "yes." When I picked up my pen and continued writing this book I had placed in a file many years ago, I said, "Lord, I cannot write like Alli Worthington, Lisa Whittle, or Elizabeth George." I immediately had a thought. I realized I could not, nor would ever be able to write like them. So, I gave up on that idea and started writing what He placed in my heart to share. I thought about Moses in the Old Testament, who reminded God of his speech impediment when God asked him to lead the Israelites out of Egypt. I, too, have given Him excuses for not doing something He has spoken to me to accomplish. Immediately I began to think about the scripture where God told Moses that He did not need his mouth; He would use what was in his hand. God will use whatever gift, talent, ability, or person for His glory. He has placed dreams in each of us. It is time we surrender to Him, allow Him to work in us and through us, and use the time we have left in our one precious life.

## Seeds of His Presence

God speaks to you through His word, plants seeds of possibility, and speaks to us through His presence. Because He speaks to us, daily devotions and church attendance are so important. When we are in His presence, He speaks. In your quiet times and the moments when thoughts enter your mind about specific areas in your life, I call these a "word from the Lord." I have never heard His audible voice, but I have felt His presence and believe with every fiber of my being that He works through and in us when we are open to His will. The Lord will give you a word about your marriage, home, kids, job, etc., if you can listen to His voice.

He has spoken to my spirit multiple times throughout my life. I have heard his call. I have answered "yes" to whatever He has for my life except for once. And I will never forget that "once." He led me to a huge decision, and I gave Him all the reasons I could not do it. We were driving through Nashville, TN, and in the vehicle, I felt Him in my spirit say, "ok." For weeks nothing was in my mind about what He was leading me to do. I begged Him to reveal and begin to work. I promised Him I would do what He had asked, but nothing ever developed from my "yes, Lord, but" mentality. It took almost three years for Him to move in the direction I knew was right. This time, the first mention from my husband of a ministry move, I was all in. This was it. Afraid? Absolutely! But, this time, I was more afraid of never hearing His voice again or feeling His presence in my spirit directing me to take a risk. No risk, no reward. I knew I was one decision from a different life. But, this time, I knew He was giving me a second chance I had been praying for. This time my answer was, "Yes,

Lord!" He will lead and guide you, and in one moment, the peace of God will pass all understanding, keeping your heart and mind on Him (Phil. 4:16-17).

## Seeds of Provision

Shortly after my "all-in moment" with the Lord, our family made plans to move to another city. I had peace as we placed our "For Sale" sign in front of the houses where our children grew up. I struggled with the security found in the place for a long while. I now had the security of being in His perfect will and knowing He would be magnified and praised wherever we live. Several days passed, and no one viewed our home or property. Finally, one afternoon when the boys were away at ball practices, I had an hour alone. I feel on my face in the living room, begging the Lord to provide a way for us to follow His direction. No sooner had I gotten off my knees than a family was at the front door inquiring about the house. He once again had heard my plea.

Shortly after, we made a massive move to the inner city. With the anticipation of ministry employment, we packed up our lives and moved. Our family and friends were not too encouraging. Frankly, they thought we were crazy. My sweet husband says it was our "Red Sea Moment." Like Moses, we had to walk through the dry ground. I prayed, trusted His provisions, and followed what the Lord prepared for our family. My husband and I both felt the Lord moving us in this direction.

We were obedient and excited to be a part of His plan. But, within a week of arriving, our jobs were no longer available, and everything fell apart. Life as we knew it began to unravel. What started as a "Red Sea Moment" began to feel like an "Abraham moment." No plan, no securities, just blind faith. However, God worked mightily in that season of our lives.

I have so many answered prayers journaled, and I can smile today knowing we came out on the other side closer to Jesus than ever before and alive. I will always remember one answered prayer that I would be telling anyone who doubts hearing direction from the Lord or the power of prayer. God provided a job for my husband, and I began teaching piano lessons to make ends meet. Once, we had no money or food to finish the week before payday. I shared my concern with my husband, and we prayed, claiming Psalms 37:25. "I have been young, and now am old, but have never seen the righteous forsaken or his seed (children) begging bread." I prayed again and reminded God that we had four sons, and they liked eating. I thanked Him for what He would do and how I would be praising Him for the rest of my life for taking care of us. I read 2 Samuel 22:33, telling God my strength is to trust Him in all things.

Within the hour, I heard a knock at our door. A new friend I had met at church was standing on the other side with bags. I opened the door, and she said with a smile, "The bread shop down the street received an extra load of bread, which was on sale, super cheap. Can you all use some delicious bread?" In addition to the bread, she also shared fresh eggs. At that moment, I knew He was directing my life. The Lord took care of us that day and every day after that. I will never forget that day.

Months passed, and God opened another door for our family. It was not a "Red Sea Moment" like before, but a moment only He could have provided. It was our moment to be all in with God's direction for our lives. We moved to another city and began ministering again. Here we have seen many things that would not be possible if we had not obeyed His voice and followed Him leading to the inner city. Corrie TenBoon said, "Heaven has no panic; Heaven has plans." Heaven has plans for your life! One life is all we have. We either use it or lose it. Let's make it count!

**What is one deliberate decision you can make today that will change your life?**

*We plant, we water, we wait, and then we harvest! Water the seeds that mean the most to you!*

# Chapter 10

Don't Quit - Water the Seeds of Perseverance

*Let us not become weary in well doing, for at the proper time, we will reap a harvest if we do not give up. – Galatians 6:9 ESV*

To persevere means to continue in the course of action, even if it's difficult. The Apostle Paul reminds us in I Corinthians 9:24-27 that running the race of life is not about standing strong but moving forward. Doing something is a significant part of perseverance, no matter how hard or long it takes to reach a goal. Living out our lives intentionally does not just happen. It takes perseverance. In this perseverance, we must be intentional, showing up for what we hoped to be true and continue living each day to its fullest. We must get up each day and live the lives we truly want. Things will never be perfect, but living life daily, anticipating the Lord to do great and mighty things in us and through us, is well spent.

## Seeds of Action

As a woman, you must not let the unnecessary distractions of the world cause you to be hateful or indifferent. My mother was good at not sweating small things when I was young. Her example, compassion, direction, and leadership of our home were breathtaking. I observed as she read "How To" books, went to the library, studied child development, led Bible study, and encouraged others. No matter how difficult the day had been, going home was like having a tiny part of Heaven here on Earth. Her positive attitude and "never lose heart speeches" are still woven in my spirit today as an adult. She is still the glue that holds us together. Every day I want to be like her. But, in truth, some days are easier than others when it comes to persevering. Think about your home. What would these individuals say about you? Are you a blessing? An encouragement? Or do you allow the world's distractions to make you unpleasant to be around?

I once heard the story of a young mother walking into the grocery store with her three-year-old girl. As they walked passed the deli, the little girl asked for cookies, and the mother said, "Not today." The little girl began to cry. "Now Stacy, we only have half the aisles to go through, don't be upset. It won't be long". Soon they came to the candy aisle, and the little girl began to beg for candy. When the mother said she could not have any, the little girl started to cry again. Finally, the mother said, "There, there, Stacy, only two more aisles to go, and we will be checking out." When they got to the checkout, the little girl threw a tantrum. The mother patiently said, "Stacy, in five minutes, we will be through the checkout lane and then go home and take a nice nap." As they exited the store, a man followed her to the parking lot. He said, "I couldn't help but notice how patient you are with Stacy. You are a good mother." The lady laughed and said, "My little girl's name is Anna. I'm Stacy." When I finished listening to this, I couldn't help but smile. If there's anything the world needs today, it is ladies who are full of grace and patience.

## Seeds of Intentions

Throughout my years, I've noted two kinds of people worldwide. Those that wait on something to happen and those that make it happen. I choose to be the latter. We must learn to live beyond the way we feel. Some days I wouldn't say I like doing my routines and investing in people. If I have not had a break or rest days, I find time to rest, get back up, and start again. If you need a break, take it. If I've had sufficient rest, I keep moving forward. You should too. Some days, we must remember that we are adults and must do things we don't necessarily want to do. Remember this is true when dealing with personal intentions or with the routines of your home and children. When raising our sons and in my day-to-day ministry interactions, I have learned that if I get upset at everything, then nothing matters! I pick and choose what upsets me. Since I rarely said "no" unless it was immoral or illegal, they could explore and branch out to whatever their hearts desired, within reason. If we always say "no" and live a daily life filled with no joy and fear of everything, this will tarnish our testimony and make us miserable. However, there were many days when I didn't feel like preparing meals or completing household chores, but I did it. I did it when I was exhausted; I did it when I was rested. No matter the kind of day I had, I would always be faithful in taking care of them. Psalms 84:11 says He is a sun and shield and will not withhold any good thing to those who walk blamelessly. I promise that if you don't hold out on the Lord, he won't hold out on you. When you are faithful to care for yourself and your families, He will honor and strengthen you as you journey each day.

## Seeds of Not Quitting

I realize life is unfair, and circumstances tend to make us bitter or hateful. Bitterness believes God got it wrong. Don't get bitter when life throws you a curve ball. Get better. Hating is like taking poison and expecting the other person to die. We cannot be bitter, hate, act as if everything causes us pain and drama, and maintain the spiritual legacy we all desire. There comes a time when we must decide that enough is enough.

I tell the devil daily that he cannot have my joy or the space in my head. It is not a rent-free zone! The devil is not welcome here. We must make the devil fight for our faith; do not give it to him. We must put one heavy foot in front of the other with love because sometimes faith is that simple. When we begin to waiver or want to quit, we must send everything out of our minds. We are in a fight for the hearts and souls of humanity. *Facts and failures are not final in God's kingdom!* The facts are the facts. You did what you did. I did what I did. I am where I am, and you are where you are. However, we must do everything in our power to do what must to get up and start again and keep going. I am so thankful that the person I used to be isn't the person I have to be. Quitting is not an option. In the words of Anne Shirley in *Anne of Green Gables*, "Tomorrow is always fresh with no mistakes in it."

> *Facts and failures are not final in God's kingdom!*

We cannot pray everything away by denial or close our eyes and pretend things did not happen. They did. Facts are facts. But, I must feed more than facts to my spirit. My faith must be in Christ Jesus, the author, and finisher of my faith. Phillippians 1:6 tells us to be confident that He who began a good work in us will complete it. Paul did not doubt that God would finish the good work He had begun in their lives; we should not doubt it either.

## Seeds of Getting Along with Others

A part of walking and living a life filled with perseverance is the wisdom to work well with others. Elizabeth Elliot reminds us, "Never pass up an opportunity to keep your mouth shut." Unfortunately, this is one thing I've learned from experience. People are not always easy to get along with. However, don't give up! Galatians 6:9 tells us not to give up doing good. Loving God, loving people, loving those around you, and being like Jesus are key principles constantly on my mind as an I move throughout each day. I learned long ago that individuals do not want to be controlled, just influenced. I've encountered numerous personalities in my many years of ministry, and I am smart enough to know I can be right or be like Jesus. Many times I've shared my faith and then just walked away. I can not force the gospel nor make individuals live life intentionally. Neither can you.

## Seeds of God's Presence

Looking back on my life, the best parts have been written with persecution and pain in a place of pressure. In my early 40s, my life was lived from preference. Now in my early 50's, it is lived in His purpose. His purpose is more important than my plans. My intentions don't matter more than His presence. Your preferences are never more important than God's presence. His company is more valuable than any preference. If you knew the pressure I've faced in the last five years of my life, you would probably stop reading this book. My precious daddy passed away from Covid in 2021. This was a jolt for my entire family. My daddy was our "rock," whom we all talked to and admired. He invested in people, and people knew he cared about them. He was my youth pastor as a teenager and later in my adult life; he was my pastor for all these years and my friend. His life was lived with intention, and his testimony to Jesus was beautiful. I was truly blessed to be with my daddy the day he went to Heaven. I watched him hold my mommy's hand, telling her he loved her and, without knowing it at the time, take his last breaths on Earth and step into Heaven.

It still doesn't feel real that he is not here with us. However, I am not home yet and must persevere each day, knowing that there is hope and purpose as long as there is life. I feel God's presence working daily, especially during this event. I know I will see my daddy again someday. But until then, I must continue the journey. You must know too. Even in places of pressure or hard times, I know these processes will produce something great for the purpose He has planned. So persevere, and don't give up!

## Seeds of Consistency

I had one of our sons at a specialist appointment a few years ago. The nurse and I chatted, and then the conversation turned very serious when my son shared that his mom and dad are youth/children's pastors. The nurse shared that her son attended a summer Bible camp when he was eight. When he arrived home, he announced at dinner that "Jesus died for him and that he accepted Jesus as his Savior and wanted to be baptized." The baptism happened, and life was wonderful for this mother and son. Fast forward 11 years later. He went away to university, calling home often. When the calls ceased, she began to have concerns. He was missing for six days. As campus security and friends began to look, they found her son in his dorm room. Mom shared that he passed away. With tears in her eyes, she offered no details, and I did not ask. However, she gave a beautiful testimony of God's goodness. The joy and peace on her face, her bright countenance, and the confidence in her voice are a sight I will never forget. She asked my son to go home and thank his daddy for all he did. She thanked me. With tears in her eyes, she boldly reminded us that her story would be so different if her son had not been introduced to Jesus. She was not bitter at all. Her faith reminded us that no matter what goes wrong or how horrible something may seem, it is all a part of His plan.

Don't give up. Don't quit or have a quiet quit. The term "quiet quitting" refers to individuals who show up in life but have given up or employees who put no more effort into their jobs than necessary. A quiet quit in individual life is when they quit mentally or emotionally or stop going the extra mile. A quiet quit can happen in anyone's life who chooses to continue the course of life but stops being relational and even social. Yes, we will continue caring for our children, ourselves, and even our home, but we do this with little thought or enthusiasm. We become lethargic. We are no longer invested and are still seen by others but no longer present in our hearts. Living like this is a dangerous place to be. The enemy likes a quiet quit. Take a moment and listen to "Don't Quit" by Jordan Smith. This song is on repeat in my playlist. Enjoy the journey He is paving for your destination.

**How can I persevere in my life every day in the areas HE has led me to?**

*We plant, we water, we wait, and then we harvest! Water the seeds that mean the most to you!*

# Chapter 11

Results of Faithful Watering – Growing and Reaping a Harvest Every Day!

*I have planted, Apollos watered; but God gave the increase. So then neither is he that planteth any thing, neither he that watereth, but God that giveth the increase. Now he that planteth and he that watereth are one: and every man shall receive his reward according to his labor.*
*– I Corinthians 3:6-8*

God sees the long hours and the shed tears; He knows your biggest frustrations and deepest hurts. He doesn't overlook you and does not take you for granted. Thus, the harvest will come. The symbolic meaning of harvest in the Bible surrounds two areas: God's provision for us and God's blessing for others. As believers, we experience the spirit of harvest all the time. Harvest symbolizes happiness and prosperity as we grow daily to reflect God's character in all we do. Sometimes our lives can get busy, messy, and downright bizarre. But we must never forget to keep planting and harvesting to teach and encourage the next generation to persevere in doing good, even on the hard days.

One morning, when I brushed my teeth, I mistakenly grabbed

the wrong tube and put face cream on my toothbrush! It took me a moment to realize that I wasn't tasting toothpaste! I used to think I had to have my act together for God to use me. I don't believe that anymore. I can't even put toothpaste on my toothbrush, but I know He is using me. Here's the incredible thing. He will use you, too, if you are willing. When we mess up, we get a fresh start. We all get it wrong from time to time. Yet, God is infinitely patient with us. I'm still messing up, like brushing my teeth with face cream, but He still calls me His own. He does the same for you.

*At the end of our lives, all that matters is that we finished well.* The ultimate goal of a Christian should be to hear

*At the end of our lives, all that matters is that we finished well.*

the Lord say, "Well done." So, for the rest of our days here on Earth, let's think about what we believe. We need to weed the garden of our minds and focus on growing and reaping a harvest daily!

## Seeds of Planning

The secret to a productive day usually happens before anyone else awakens or starts their day. Sometimes, I am having lunch by the time others are having breakfast. My sacred routine is how I am intentional and productive throughout the day. You do not have to do what I do, but I encourage you to have a routine. Having this cognitive rhythm will ground you. Before you are poked or pulled in different directions throughout the day, prioritize certain things. If you lose that hour in the morning doing your routine, you will spend all day looking for it.

Waking up earlier than your husband and children will give you the quiet time and jump start necessary to be intentional and have sacred daily routines and habits. You do not have to plan your day just like I do or imitate someone else's routine; you just have to have one.

A well-planned day grounds you. Before you are poked and prodded by everyone and everything that needs your attention, quiet time allows you to focus your thoughts on things that are the priority. Again, if you lose your hour in the morning, I promise you will spend all day looking for it. I have had a few mornings where I skipped this sacred hour, and I promise you that my day was not as productive and fruitful as it could have been. Morning routines kick you into momentum. If we don't start right, we will have difficulty reversing negative momentum all day. A pre-planned, disciplined, rigid, structured morning routine will liberate and free you for the rest of the day.

Please don't get hung up on what it should look like when establishing your morning rituals. As long as you have one, this is most important. It doesn't matter what this person does or that person does or thinks. Don't get hung up on specifics that others may focus on. Instead, plant your seeds. Discover what works for you. Plan what you will do every morning without fail. Make it something that you will and can do every morning without fail. Like most things in life, the key to success is in preparation. We must start planning our tomorrow the night before. Success in your daily morning routine depends on this. The hardest part about doing this simple routine is the beginning. Your brain will say and do all sorts of stuff to stop you.

## Seeds of Productivity

Get rest (see *Self Care,* Chapter 3). Quality sleep will prepare the soil of your harvest for greater things. Also, research different ways to get quality sleep/ Google it. It is vital for life! The best way to get a good night's rest is to go to bed tired. Not just mentally tired from being on a screen all day or dealing with difficult people on the job, but physically exhausted. Whether physical work from doing household chores, running to keep up with the kids, or working out, I get tired. I have been encouraged to work out at least three times per week. As we age, we must exercise to finish the last part of our lives strong. As any gardener will tell you, it takes physical strength to maintain the fields. Tend it well. Your life is your field.

Once you have had quality sleep, you need to initiate your day. Your day must start spiritually, mentally, emotionally, and physically. What you do in each of these areas is up to you. For me, jump-starting my day begins spiritually. My day begins with my alarm and my lying in bed praying about the start of my day. Communicating with Lord is the first and last thought of my day. Once I am up, I take care of my physical area. I immediately head to the kitchen and reach for my protein shake and 16 ounces of water. I then do a quick workout with stretches while the coffee is brewing.

Next, my emotional area is cultivated. I read my Bible and my devotional journal of the day. I also journal. In my journaling, I write a letter to God each morning. The ink to paper helps me leave all my anxieties and worries on the page, thus strengthening my faith journey. Next, I read my Proverb of the day (matching the month's date with the chapter in Proverbs. For example, on the second month, I read Proverbs 2). With coffee in hand, the day's message grounds me and helps me find the hope and possibilities of the day. When my emotions are reset to what is right, I can give abundantly to the world. I do this routine before I let the rest of the world in space. The world is often unkind, and everyone pulls or competes for your attention. However, when you are emotionally ready, and your plans are prepared, stress flees, and productivity flourishes. Finally, I pray from my written prayer list for at least

15 minutes. I then read 50+ pages from a preselected book. All this takes me around 90 minutes. Once this is completed, I set up for the day. Once my morning routine is complete, I only look at email, news, social media, etc. These 90 minutes are the order of my morning routine.

I must be transparent and let you know everything is complete in my bathrobe. I'm typically up at 5:30 a.m. or earlier, so by this time, it is barely 7:00 a.m., and everyone else is beginning to get up and start their day. I quickly get dressed and am now available and present for the needs of my husband and children. Morning flows are so important whether you home-educate or send your family out the door each day. Once at work or if I am home for the day, I will work another 90 minutes without email, phone, social media, etc.

Many may not be up to this challenge or think they could never establish such a schedule. Please consider it. I am living proof that it works. This method is how I raised our four sons, was home-educated, worked in ministry, and worked full- and part-time throughout my adult life. Because I have done this vigorously each day for the last 35 or more years, I am now seeing the harvest. Zig Ziglar reminds us, "Don't count the things you do. Do the things that count."

Often, we don't see the "big" picture of little things done on purpose each day. Zechariah 4:10 tells us not to despise small beginnings. Our small daily steps will soon reach our destination- a well-lived life and a legacy to future generations! Joel 1:3 "Tell your children of it, and let your children tell their children and their children and another generation."

## Seeds of Purpose

Time management is so important. Being purposeful with your time, setting boundaries around what is most important, and dreaming big are all strategies I've included in my daily life. My husband Joe always reminds me, "We are today what we are becoming." Prioritizing and disciplining yourself and your day will enable you to become what the Lord has placed you on earth for. Disciplining yourself is sacrificing the life you want right now for the life you want to live in the future. This mindset will grow your purpose.

Growing up, my parents were my biggest fans. Their encouragement to live intentionally and dream big enabled me to write and produce music before I was out of high school, teach and conduct multiple piano recitals with local students, lead a children's choir, and teach Bible studies before heading out to college. Setting goals and dreaming big continue to be a part of my daily, monthly, and yearly habits. Have all my goals been achieved? No. Have all my dreams been roses and sunshine? No. Many of my dreams in the past ten years have not come to fruition. Honestly, some days, I get tired of the cruddy place I'm in, but I remember that dreams are fertilized in stinky places. The past ten years of my life have not been the desires of my heart. However, I believe He is using the false expectations of my life to guide me into His master plan.

To make things happen, we must take risks. Sometimes those risks pay off, and success follows. Sometimes they do not, and this is ok. I Chronicles 16:27 says, "Glory and honor are in his presence every day." Start over and take more risks. When we take a chance, the Lord often uses these moments as a teachable, growing time. Every decision we make alters the future events in our lives. This is why staying near the Savior and listening to His voice is so important. Doing something scared will build confidence while walking in the truth. *Nothing great is done in the "comfort zone."* If God is leading, say "yes." Be scared for a season, but know that the fruit is amazing! I'm on the other side at 50 years old now. Remember that you can't have a harvest if you don't sow and cultivate the seed. This is true in our lives as well. I am seeing and tasting the sweet fruit from my obedience. In due time, you will too. Go and live life in full bloom.

> *Nothing great is done in the "comfort zone."*

**List one thing that you can start doing scared today.**

*We plant, we water, we wait, and then we harvest! Water the seeds that mean the most to you!*

Made in the USA
Columbia, SC
09 October 2024

3e834d34-453a-44a5-b079-35b82d0f16e5R02